LADY GAGA BORN TO BE FREE

AN UNAUTHORIZED BIOGRAPHY

LADY GAGA
BORN TO BE FREE

AN UNAUTHORIZED BIOGRAPHY

By Jake Brown

Colossus Books
An Imprint of Amber Communications Group Inc.
Phoenix   New York   Los Angeles

LADY GAGA: BORN TO BE FREE

Published by:
Colossus Books
An Imprint of Amber Communications Group Inc.
1334 East Chandler Boulevard, Suite 5-D67
Phoenix, AZ 85048
E-mail: AMBERBK@AOL.COM
WWW.AMBERBOOKS.COM

Tony Rose, Publisher/Editorial Director
Yvonne Rose, Associate Publisher
The Printed Page, Interior/Cover Design

ALL RIGHTS RESERVED

No part of this book may be reproduced or transmitted in any form or by any means—electronic or mechanical, including photocopying, recording or by any information storage and retrieval system without written permission from the authors, except for the inclusion of brief quotations in a review. Requests for permission or further information should be addressed to "The Permissions Department", Colossus Books, 1334 E. Chandler Boulevard, Suite 5-D67, Phoenix, AZ 85048, USA.

Colossus Books are available at special discounts for bulk purchases, sales promotions, fund raising or educational purposes. For details, contact: Special Sales Department, Amber Books, 1334 E. Chandler Boulevard, Suite 5-D67, Phoenix, AZ 85048, USA.

Copyright © 2014 by Jake Brown and Amber Communications Group, Inc.

Paperback ISBN # 978-1-937269-44-9
EBOOK ISBN # 978-1-937269-45-6

Library of Congress Cataloging-in-Publication Data

Brown, Jake.
  Lady Gaga : born to be free, an unauthorized biography / by Jake Brown.
      pages cm.
  Includes bibliographical references and index.
  ISBN 978-1-937269-44-9 (alk. paper)
  1. Lady Gaga. 2. Singers--United States--Biography. I. Title.
  ML420.L185B76 2014
  782.42164092--dc23
  [B]
                                        2014017005

Table of Contents:

Introduction: Meet Lady Gaga	1
Photo Journey One: The Early Years	6
Chapter 1: "Gaga from Birth"	15
Chapter 2: 176 Stanton Street	29
Chapter 3: "F.A.M.E."	41
Chapter 4: "Little Monsters"	55
Chapter 5: "The Fame Monster E.P."	63
Photo Journey Two: Career on the Rise	70
Chapter 6: "Born This Way"	79
Chapter 7: Gaga Takes Over the World…	95
Chapter 8: Life as a Fashion Show…	105
Chapter 9: ARTPOP	119
Photo Journey Three: International Superstar	142
Conclusion: 2014 and Beyond…	151

Dedication

This book is dedicated to my dear friend Helen Watts,
who introduced me to Lady Gaga
and is the biggest 'Little Monster' I know. ☺

Thank You(s):

First and foremost, thank you to my beautiful wife Carrie. To my wonderful parents James and Christina Brown for your continued belief in my creative pursuits, and to Josh for being the best brother (and Best Man re the pending nuptials J) I could ask for; the extended Thieme and Brown families; my AWESOME pets, the Hanneman and Scooter; my squad of amazing friends that hold me down year after year for the past 25: Alex (and Ellen, Jackson and Willamina) Schuchard, Andrew (and Sarah) McDermott, Cris Ellauri (and family), 'The' Sean Fillinich, Adam (and Shannon) Perri, Bob (and Cayenne) O'Brien, Paul & Helen Watts, Richard (and Lisa & Regan) Kendrick, Alexandra Federov (and my man Larry, thank you); my amazingly talented engineer Aaron Harmon (congrats on all Basecamp's success) and thank you for helping me bring my own songs to life on record over the past 5 years and as many albums finally coming in 2014); Joe Viers; Catherine and Freddy Powers; Joe Satriani and Mick Brigden for the wild ride that has been co-writing Strange Beautiful Music!; Kenny Aronoff for the amazing opportunity to co-write your memoirs; MVD Music Distribution (Ed Seamen, Eve, Dave, Sabrina, et all); Dave and Janne at Morphius; and finally the other amazing publishers I have had the privilege of working with over the past 12 years and 35 books: Tony & Yvonne Rose at Amber Books; John Cerullo et all at Hal Leonard; Glenn Yeffeth et all at BenBella Books; Jack David, Crissy, et all at ECW Press; John Blake Publishing (UK); Cherry Red Books (UK); BearManor Media; SCB Distribution; and all my Facebook peeps…

Lady Gaga: Born to be Free

"You are not at all what I expect—you are much more…"
—Barbara Walters on Lady Gaga

"She has been compared to another ground breaking female artist known for visuals, music and stage shows, like Madonna, of course."
—Lady Gaga to Larry King

Introduction
Meet Lady Gaga

Lady Gaga is her generation's Madonna. Hailed as "the first true millennial superstar" by Billboard, who credited the pop superstar as "an artist who specialized in re-purposing the past—particularly the '80s—for present use, creating sustainable pop for a digital world, Gaga mastered, the constant connection of the internet era, Gaga generated countless mini sensations through her style, her videos, and her music, cultivating a devoted audience."

Speaking much in the spirit of Madonna's declaration in 1983 during her first appearance on Dick Clark's American Bandstand when she declared that "I want to rule the world," Gaga would achieve just that within the first four years of her ascension to the top of pop.

In authenticating her heir apparency as her generation's Queen of Pop, Vanity Fair reminded its readers in a 2012 cover story that it "in the mere four years that she's had a recording contract, Gaga, now 25, has become a global phenomenon. She was No. 11 on last year's Forbes list of the "World's 100 Most Powerful Women", coming in ahead of Oprah Winfrey.

She has sold a total of 23 million albums and 63 million singles worldwide. Her net worth has been reported to be over $100 million. Her sophomore album, Born This Way, sold more than 1.1 million copies in its first week of release, last May. She performed for 2.4 million people in 202 shows in 28 countries on the year-and-a-half-long Monster Ball Tour. She has more than 44.5 million 'Likes' on Facebook, and more than 15 million people follow her on Twitter."

Up to 20 million + followers by 2014, Lady Gaga declared to The Guardian of her own blonde ambitions that "I am taking it to another level…Fame is not pretending to be rich, it's carrying yourself in a way that exudes confidence and passion for music or art or fishing or whatever the hell it is that you're passionate about, and projecting yourself in a way that people say, 'Who the fuck is that?' It has nothing to do with money. I can wear a $2 pair of pants and a T-shirt and a pair of sunglasses for two bucks on the street, but I can make it look like I'm Paris Hilton. You gotta have the fame, you gotta exude that thing. You gotta make people care, you gotta know and believe how important you are. You gotta have conviction in your ideas."

Savvy maker and marketer of her own image, The Guardian in their front-page feature on the singer as she took Britain by storm, noted that "the crucial thing about Lady GaGa is that she sees herself as not just another pop muppet, but as a living, breathing work of art…(She) insists that not only are her songs inextricably linked to their performance and to her life in general, but also that she is doing something tangibly different from anything ever done before." The LA Times highlighted another important distinction from Gaga's pop peers in why she has successfully maintained such a baseline of originality throughout her career "she not only reiterates her assertion of total originality but also finesses it until it's both a philosophical stance about how constructing a persona from pop-cultural sources can be an expression of a person's truth."

Painting an even more honest picture about why she felt fans bought so authentically into her brand, Gaga confessed to Vogue that "the truth is, the mystery and the magic is my art. That is what I am good at. You are fascinated with precisely the thing that you are trying to analyze and undo." Taking advantage of the fluidity within popular trends to constantly stay on its cutting edge, Gaga operated from a philosophy where "I think pop is ever changing," explaining to Popdust.com that "I hope to death it never stops being so. Art is designed to be different from moment to moment, and songs should reflect that. They shouldn't all be the same. That's my ambition as an artist. I'm not particularly obsessed with how my career will be viewed when it's over. I'm much more obsessed with what I create along the way and how dedicated I am to each creation."

Projecting a confidence she hoped to inspire in each and every one of her fans, Gaga's fans were equally drawn to her fearlessness as a superstar, boldly and convincingly arguing to Vogue in 2012 that "speaking purely from a musical standpoint, I think I am a great performer. I am a talented entertainer. I consider myself to have one of the greatest voices in the industry. I consider myself to be one of the greatest songwriters. I wouldn't say that I am one of the greatest dancers, but I am really quite good at what I do…I think it's OK to be confident in yourself." Building a bond of support between herself and her fans utilizing social media as a global network within which to spread her message and amass an army of 'Little Monsters'—as she affectionately called them—to the tune of over 20 million Twitter followers in less than 5 years, the LA Times honed in on Gaga's talent for tapping "into one of the primary obsessions of our age—the changing nature of the self in relation to technology, the ever-expanding media sphere, and that sense of always being in character and publicly visible that Gaga calls 'the fame'—and made it her own obsession, the subject of her songs and the basis of her persona."

Agreeing in 2012 that this was the time to make the most of her momentum, Gaga waxed poetic on the subject of why she had earned that capital with Rolling Stone Magazine, proudly acknowledging that "I *have* attention," before posing the more important question in retort to one from RS regarding why: "Is it that you believe that I am attention-seeking or shock for shock's sake, or is it just that it's been a long time since someone has embraced the art form the way that I have? Perhaps it's been a couple of decades since there's been an artist that's been as vocal about culture, religion, human rights, and politics.

I'm so passionate about what I do, every bass line, every EQ. Why is it that you don't want more from the artist, why is it that you expect so little, so when I give and give, you assume it's narcissistic?"

True that many pop stars before her had fallen victim to becoming lost in their own limelight, Gaga preferred to use hers as a guiding one for her fans to follow by example, telling Barbara Walters that "I aspire to try to be a teacher to my young fans," adding to Vogue on the same topic that "I want for people in the universe, my fans and otherwise, to essentially use me as an escape. I am the jester to the kingdom. I am the route out. I am the excuse to explore your identity. To be exactly who you are and to feel unafraid. To not judge yourself, to not hate yourself. Because, as funny as it is that I am on the cover of Vogue—and no one is laughing harder than I am!"

While she had to shake her head once in a while in disbelief at the worldwide phenomenon she'd become in such record time by typical popstar standards, Gaga was quick to reassure her fans and critics alike not to mistake this humility for a step backward where her ambition to achieve even greater heights was concerned, declaring boldly to The Guardian that "I don't wanna be one song. I wanna be the next 25 years of pop music. But it's really hard to measure that kind of ambition. That kind of blonde ambition is looked at with a raised brow, because most artists don't have longevity today."

Taking care to make clear she wanted to blaze that trail based on her own legacy, the superstar affirmed to the LA Times that "I don't see myself as an heir," Gaga revealed in a conversation with Popdust.com regarding her strategy for staying relevant as a trend-setter throughout the inevitable shifts that pop music/culture trends that can turn a pop sensation obsolete overnight that perhaps her greatest "challenge is…what others view as artifice—my wigs, my makeup, my clothes, my love for show business and theater—to me, these are the paint in my palette. These things are not artifice. These things are my reality.

But they create a boundary between me and the public, which I have to fight through. People wonder, *Is she for real? Is it all an act?* But my question is, *Since when did the act become a bad thing?* Show business has always been about the act. Hasn't it?"

Stefani Germanotta Early Years
Lady Gaga—Childhood Photos

Stefani with her mother Cynthia Germanotta and baby sister Natali

Stefani preparing one day to be LADY GAGA

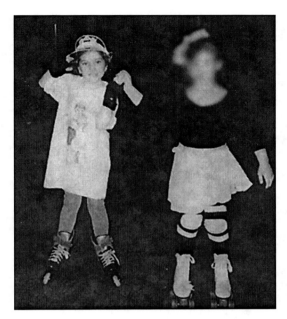

Stefani with a friend at the roller rink

Stefani with childhood friends dressed up

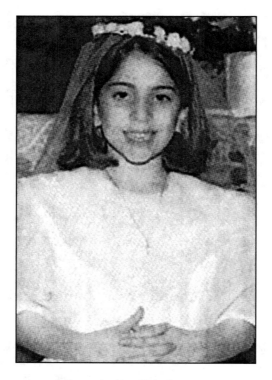

Stefani at her First Holy Communion

Stefani playing piano at an early age

Meet Lady Gaga

The future star Stefani at a high school dance with her dad Joe Germanotta in 2004

Lady Gaga: Born to be Free

Lady Gaga Early Years
A Genius Emerges

A Genius Emerges—Stefani's "like a guy" look

A Genius Emerges—bare faced beauty

Meet Lady Gaga

Stefani the Starlett

Stefani the Diva In Dreads

Meet Stefani the Princess

Lady Gaga with Lady Starlight

Lady Gaga girls night out

Lady Gaga: Born to be Free

Lady Gaga with her parents—Cynthia and Joe Germanotta

Lady Gaga and her sister Natali

"Ever since we were kids, my parents gave us the freedom to be ourselves…"
—Natali Germanotta, Lady Gaga's Younger Sister,
Teen Vogue

"I was a strange, loud little kid who could sit at the piano and kill a Beethoven piece."
—Lady Gaga to *Vogue*, 2012

Chapter 1
Gaga from Birth

Beyond their professional parallels, Lady Gaga and Madonna ironically shared in several key pieces of personal pedigree, beginning with the fact that both pop stars grew up in strict Italian Catholic homes with very identifiable Italian last names, Madonna Louise Ciccone for the latter pop icon's obvious namesake, and in Gaga's case, Stefani Joanne Angelina Germanotta.

Born on March 28th, 1986 to Joseph and Cynthia Germanotta, New York Magazine reported in a cover story on Gaga's upbringing that the future superstar "grew up in a duplex on the Upper West Side, on one of the eclectic blocks between Columbus and Amsterdam in the West Seventies that are a mix of prewar brownstones, tenements, and modern condos. Her father ran a company that installed Wi-Fi in hotels, and her mother worked for a time as a V.P. at Verizon."

An individualist in every sense of the word who stood facing stage-to-crowd from the time she could first stand, Gaga once quipped to Elle of her role as a natural performer that "I was always in a show. I was just such an over-the-top crazypants," an early sign of what she later told Larry King was "my destiny to be a performer. I used to perform even just in restaurants with my family or in the living room." Demonstrating not only her natural promise as a performer while still running around in diapers, Gaga showed early signs of her musical talents as well, revealing to Songwriter's Universe that "my mom told me that I just basically hoisted myself up on a piano seat, and I used to always try to play, I think I always had a strong pull to music." Gaga would combine her already-ambition talents as a musician and performer for the first time publicly at the age of 8 at a piano recital, sharing her memory with New York Magazine that "there was a line of twenty girls sitting in a row in our pretty dresses, and we each got up to play, I did a really good job. I was quite good."

Chiming in proudly with their own memories—as her first fans—of recognizing their child's talent stood out beyond a simple talent, father Joseph Germanotta confirmed to Vanity Fair that "we wouldn't have encouraged her to pursue this if we didn't think she had the talent," adding that the decision was made that much easier by the fact that "she was just determined." Writing her first song ahead of entering her teen years, mother Cynthia Germanotta was equally inspired by daughter Stefani's dedication to practice and her work ethic in general, recalling with admiration to the Daily Beast that "she was always extremely driven, extremely hardworking. If she had to go to a voice lesson and her friends wanted to hang out, they wouldn't always understand. With her, it was a passion. Not a hobby."

An important part of her early musical education would play out at home as her mother and father opened Stefani's ears to a melting pot of musical influences that would reflect vividly in her later albums of original material, rooted in moments like the one when, as a young child, "my parents got me Stevie Wonder's 'Signed, Sealed, Delivered' and The Beatles when I was younger." To MTV that they represented "good choices, mom and dad!" One head-turning artist who had a heavy impact on Gaga as a fledgling songwriter was none other than the legendary BOSS from neighboring New Jersey, Bruce Springsteen, whose presence as a songwriter "had such an influence on our home...my dad was in a Bruce Springsteen cover band for many years. He was a real Jersey Shore boy and...gave me, I believe it was for Christmas, a Bruce Springsteen songbook for the piano, it was 'Thunder Road,' which is my favorite Bruce Springsteen song. My dad said, 'If you learn how to play this song we will take out a loan for a grand piano, a baby grand.'

So I remember it was the hardest thing for me. I was playing these huge (classical) pieces, like 15 pages long, and then there was this Bruce Springsteen song. I opened up the book and there was like chords, guitar chords. I was so confused. I didn't understand it, so I just started to read it and eventually, eventually I got it down." Songwriter Universe added of other pivotal rock arena influences that arrived in Gaga's ear courtesy of her father's influence that "passion grew exponentially and she was encouraged by her father, who used to play her records by Springsteen, Queen, David Bowie and Elton John, who became her artistic influences."

Elaborating on the growth of her musical talent in real time with the expansion of her exposure to new musical styles—ones she absorbed personally on a musical level as a player throughout her formative years—Gaga shared with ShowStudio.com that after "*I started out when I was really young so I was playing classical music when I was 4, when I turned 11 I started to write pop music, then I started playing jazz and wrote some jazz records. Then I got into ragtime, then I got into folk jam music (Bob Dylan), then I got into Queen and Bowie and rock 'n' roll, then I started listening to disco. I guess you could say it was my intellectual evolution. My love of music began to change and form when I was living downtown alone. I was able to more confidently look into myself and ask the question—must I write? Must I create* music? I answered—I must. If you must create music, what must you say? Why make it at all? I resigned myself to making the kind of music I wanted to listen to, not the most credible or notable. What I wanted to listen to, what I thought was great, what could be groundbreaking where I was living. Where indie music was much more popular, pop music was classed as corporate and unimportant. I decided, in true Gaga style, to be revolutionary: go against the grain."

Growing up as a child against the musical backdrop of the 1990s, Gaga identified her place among the stars early on, confessing in the same conversation to the truth that *"always knew it was my destiny to be an entertainer; I was ready to be the new thing. I always admired the women that I grew up watching, all the pop stars: Britney and Christina, I was a big Laila Kane fan—Madonna, Blondie, Patty Smith, Linda Perry and Four Non-Blondes. I could go on and on and on about so many but I guess I'm speaking specifically about the 90s—I was four in 1990—I'm speaking specifically until I was about fifteen which would mean I was in my younger years. Around thirteen I was into older music—Zeppelin, Pink Floyd, Queen. I went through a transition—I was much more obsessed with male rock stars, at a point. I didn't identify with women as much in the 90's—I was more obsessed with men. Grunge, Kurt Cobain—I loved so many kinds of music. A female figure—I was too young to know what I could become—but here we are."*

During these crucial early years of her first exposures to the derivative influences that would help shape her as an artist throughout the years to come, a young Stefani would find herself equally drawn to both the musical and performance sides of being an entertainer. In this way, Gaga's heavy emphasis on theatrics within her elaborate cabaret-esque live stage shows in later years became a natural extension of her childhood enchantment with musical theatre, sharing in a conversation with Larry King years later that her molding began once again at home, recalling that *"my mother was actually in musical theater when she was younger."*

Tracing her first exposure to live performance altogether in an interview with Harper's Bazaar in 2014 back to childhood when "I went to see *Phantom of the Opera* with my grandma and my mom when I was very little. The stage, the voice, the *music*? Composer Andrew Lloyd Webber has been a massive inspiration to me for some time—the storytelling, that deliciously somber undertone in his music. I just knew that he could *see* it while he was creating it. It is the same way I experience music…*Romeo & Juliet*—both the Shakespeare and the Baz (Luhrmann) versions I was, also, changed by profoundly as a child."

Attending Saturday acting classes from the age of 11, Gaga years later still relished her vivid memory of "the first time that I drank out of an imaginary coffee cup. That's the very first thing they teach you. I can feel the rain, too, when it's not raining." Inspired from a royal perspective by her mother's fondness for the Princess of Wales, an iconic symbol of British aristocratic elegance that Gaga would later reflect in costume designs for her stage show, sharing her memory with Larry King in 2010 that "I love Princess Diana. So much. She has—was an enormous influence on me when I was younger because my mother worshipped her so much. Her story, how she began, what she married into, how her society affected her as a woman. I was always very fascinated with Princess Diana. When she died, it was—I'll never forget. My mother was crying, sitting on the couch watching the news, and I was very young. And it was this very powerful moment in my childhood watching my mother so connected to someone. So I guess you could say she is one of my biggest icons. As well as, you know, David Bowie, wonderful."

Determined, along with her independent musical and theatrical tutelage, to make sure their daughter received the most rounded education possible, at age 12, Stefani's parents enrolled her in the prestigious Convent of the Sacred Heart. A private school located on Manhattan's Upper East Side on 91st street, according to the school's website, "inherent in what makes Sacred Heart unique is a rich history that began at the turn of the 19th century. In 1800,

St. Madeleine Sophie Barat founded the Society of the Sacred Heart in France, with the singular—and revolutionary—goal of educating women. Her vision of personal growth in an atmosphere of wise freedom continues to guide us today. Convent of the Sacred Heart at 91st Street is part of a worldwide Network of Sacred Heart schools. Our Goals and Criteria, derived from St. Madeleine Sophie's original concept of an ideal education, form the framework of our educational philosophy. As they have for over 200 years, Sacred Heart women positively influence the world by thinking critically, acting with courage and compassion, and manifesting an informed and lively faith. In addition to a rigorous and challenging curricular program for girls from pre-k through grade 12, we are a community of individuals all working together to help form the 'whole child,' addressing her intellectual, spiritual, social and emotional development."

Eager to sow both her dramatic oats and those of her hormones as a young teenage girl beginning to go through the early stages of coming into womanhood, upon enrolling in her new school, New York Magazine reported that "by eighth grade, she had also realized that acting was a way to meet boys and began auditioning for plays with Sacred Heart's brother school, Regis High School, on 84th Street, near Park Avenue. She always landed the lead: Adelaide in *Guys and Dolls,* Philia in *A Funny Thing Happened on the Way to the Forum.*" Confirming that landing her first lead, as Adelaide, was a monumental early moment of triumph for Gaga's confidence as a performer, she mused years later in an interview with Digital Spy that when "I got cast as Adelaide, it was the greatest moment of high school. I tell you, I still dream about it."

While she found her escape in theatre, Gaga found herself battling from day one to conform to the school's conservative aspects, especially where her flamboyant fashion sensibility was choked by what classmate Cristina Civetta described years later as a regimen of etiquette that began from the moment "when we were dropped off at school in the morning…(and) a Sister would greet us at the entrance and we had to curtsy to her. In the lower school, we had to wear a grey tunic over which we wore red-and-white checked pinafores, and blue shorts underneath everything for modesty. In the upper school, we wore blue cotton skirts in summer and a kilt in winter, and they had a yardstick to make sure they were the correct length…They blasted us with religion but we also got an insanely good education. We had to go to mass in the chapel every Friday and a Wednesday morning prayer meeting."

Gaga—years before she was embraced into popularity on a world level—battled social rejection from classmates in a theme all-too-ironically-common to many celebrities who suffered extreme loneliness as adolescents, outcast from popularity or mainstream acceptance of any kind within the kind of local social arena Gaga was playing at the time. Driving home the true severity of her situation in a conversation years later with Larry King, Stephani candidly confessed that during "my childhood in school, and for a very long time, I used to always feel like such a freak. I didn't have very many friends in school. I had a few close friends. And I—I wasn't a popular girl. And got made fun of every day and couldn't really relate to anyone and didn't want do dress like anyone else and liked different things. And I related to men more than I related to women. And I felt like a freak, and I had nowhere to go."

Reading much like an after-school T.V. movie about bullying, Lady Gaga starred in exactly that kind of drama throughout this sad time socially, revealing to The Guardian years after the fact that, for precisely the same reasons she's embraced today, back then, because "I'm eccentric and talkative and audacious and theatrical…I used to get picked on. I got thrown in a trash can on a street corner once by some boys who were hanging out with girls in my class… (I felt) worthless. Embarrassed. Mortified. I was 14. Three boys put me in it. The girls were laughing when they did it…I got profanity written all over my locker at school and all the others were nice and clean. I got pinched in the hallways and called a slut," adding in an equally as cruel memory to Rolling Stone Magazine that she was "being teased for being ugly, having a big nose, being annoying, 'Your laugh is funny, you're weird, why do you always sing, why are you so into theater, why do you do your make-up like that?'...I used to be called a slut, be called this, be called that, I didn't even want to go to school sometimes."

Things got so bad, Gaga shared with the New York Times that "I was called really horrible, profane names very loudly in front of huge crowds of people, and my schoolwork suffered at one point. I didn't want to go to class. And I was a straight-A student, so there was a certain point in my high school years where I just couldn't even focus on class because I was so embarrassed all the time. I was so ashamed of who I was."

Being rejected at school caused Stephani to naturally lash out at home, confirming to Elle Magazine that "I was quite a rebel at home...(because) I was bullied at school. I was called 'Rabbit Teeth' and 'Big Nose' and 'Dyke'. I would stay up all night studying Latin and blow-drying my hair and I would do a full face of makeup before I went to bed so I could wake up and go straight to school. I was so dressed-up for class and it was an all-girls school, so some of the students thought it was a bit ridiculous, I suppose. Maybe my creativity came off a bit strange. But the worst form of bullying is where everyone gets invited to a party except for you. What did you do this weekend? 'Well, what did you do? Did you hear about Friday?' It's cruel, it's mean, everyone talking about the weekend and you've got nothing to say, nothing to contribute, cos you're left out and excluded...I never made a separation between what I put on in the morning and who I am. So it was challenging for me to try and understand why people were being so vicious about me being myself...I was being poked and probed and people would actually touch me and touch my clothes and be like, 'What the fuck is that,' just so awful."

Arguably creating her pre-fame star persona as a defense mechanism of sorts, a rejection to the rejection itself she experienced in the highschool halls, Gaga confirmed years later to Time Magazine in 2012 that "my courage and the value it had as a child was one of the reasons that made me be pursued. Something like, 'Who do you think you are?'"

Nurtured at home by her always-accepting parents, who encouraged Stephani to embrace her artistic personality as it began to flourish in development during these crucial formative years, the singer's mother Cynthia Germanotta recalled that "we had a long conversation about it…We just allowed her to follow her creativity. Generally, I was pretty independent and driven myself. We're like that as a family. Our mentality is to be strong…We talked about how it affected her, about how important it is to be inclusive. She was always one to include people, sitting with new people in school at lunch."

Rightfully still disgusted years later by her daughter's treatment during those precious teenage years, Stefani Germanotta felt that Gaga's treatment came "down to meanness and cruelty (and) exclusion is a form of that," with the singer discovering that among the other impacts this rejection had on her psyche as a woman at the time, "it took me a long time to feel sexy because I was bullied at school." Reflecting back on the longer-term effects of the trauma of her highschool years, even as it motivated her to push that much harder for fame, Gaga told Time Out London in 2011 that "being bullied stays with you your whole life, and no matter how many people are screaming your name or how many Number One hits you have, you can still wake up and feel like a loser."

Gaga drew greatly during this challenging time in her life from the well of strength her mother and grandmother provided as inspiring examples of strong women, reasoning in an interview with Time Magazine that "my mother and I are very close…You only need one person, someone who believes in you," adding to ShowStudio.com that her Grandmothers both served as strong pillars of support and strength as well, recalling that "*both my grandmothers:*

my mother's side and my father's side. They are so strong, they've been through so much and they both came from nothing. They are just the strongest, most irreplaceable women, so deeply loved by their husbands, as well. I find this fascinating and impossible—to be such a strong woman and to find a man that will love you without making himself feel insecure—impossible. Both my grandmothers and my mother have done that. I suppose the three—the trinity of women in my life—have been the most interesting. I suppose they're also the reason I'm a feminist. It's quite crazy that I'm a feminist but what's so lovely about it is that so many people misinterpret feminism as man hating: it has nothing to do with that. I really admire my grandmothers and my mom. I think an interesting person is someone that teaches you something about your life."

Clearly grateful for her parents' rock of support throughout these tumultuous social years, Lady Gaga proudly declared in 2010 reflecting back that "*my mother and father are the most giving, wonderful, Christian people—no judgment. They taught my sister and I to be so free in our judgment. There's such a diluted sense of religion and what is right. Perhaps the school's just not what it used to be. It makes me very, very sad. I have to just be honest about something so personal. I don't want to lie, the truth is my closest friends and family have been so wonderful. I'm so grounded, I'm myself, I don't give a shit about money or yachts or big houses or fucking dinner parties. I think it's really wrong to judge people. It's really wrong to place a social importance on a family or human being. I'd never do that to someone, it's everything I'm against. I have to be honest about it, it's how I truly feel. My sister is the most wonderful, precious person. I will say the teachers at the school are the best and the most wonderful teachers. They are truly magical. Sister Bio, Mrs. Price, Doctor Lampidas—just so many wonderful, wonderful teachers.*"

While she still held her school in high regard years later, she clearly didn't feel the same way about many of the aforementioned classmates who made her high school social life a living hell, happy to leave them in the stardust, quipping triumphantly to Showstudio.

com *"my classmates, I don't really speak to all of them but my closest girlfriends are wonderful and haven't changed a bit. As for the school, that has been a bit more of a sad experience for me. The teachers have been wonderful but not the administration of the school, many of which I don't really know. The nuns that used to run the school that I still know were lovely and they love me—especially the English teachers and the head of the school I was close with. They were wild feminists and instilled so much good wisdom in us. I have nothing bad to say about where I went to school. They really gave us such a wonderful education. I've been really sad about some of the things that have happened with my high school because my sister goes there.*

My family worked so hard: my parents were not rich, they spent every dollar they made on me and my sister going to the most wonderful, expensive private school that they could afford because they wanted us to have the opportunities that they didn't have. I suppose in an attempt to also say something about religion, as a Catholic school I've been slightly put off by the very un-Catholic way they have responded to my success and how supportive my family has been of the school for over 20 years. I don't like to say bad things but it's been sad, I have such a lovely memory of my schooling and I know how my parents didn't have things because they wanted my sister and I to have things. The way my family has been treated has really made me sad because they gave the school everything so that my sister and I could have a wonderful education. Every charity, every auction, every time the chapel needed refurnishing, they were so giving."

With the judgment she battled no doubt an extension of the spoiled children of New York's wealthiest families she shared classrooms with throughout high school, she pointed in an interview with DJ Ron Slomowicz to one poignant example of attending school with the Hilton Sisters, recalling that "I went with Nicky. Paris, I believe, left and went to Dwight. But, you know, it's impressive to be that perfect all the time, these girls. I was always a weird girl in school, who did theatre and came to school with lots of red lipstick on or my hair perfectly curled, or whatever I was doing to get attention. It's funny as it's almost like they were there to make me aware, because so much of what I do now is that I try to twist my world into the commercial community. So I guess they've been quite an influence on me. Not them in particular, but the idea of the self-proclaimed artist."

Serving in an ironic way to introduce Gaga to the highline world of fashion via clothing and make-up accessories her family couldn't afford to buy her with the tight budget they stuck strictly to where Stefani remembered "all our money went into education and the house."

Still, Gaga found a way to immerse herself in the fantasy of high-end fashion, beginning with her discovery of the teenage refuge the local M.A.C. make-up store became for her, sharing her memory with CNN of being "a huge fan of M.A.C. since I was very young. M.A.C. is a lifestyle. M.A.C. is sort of this—this place and this mecca near my house where I knew I could be whoever I wanted to be and really find myself as an individual and feel confident and secure…"I was so excited because all the girls at Sacred Heart always had their fancy purses, and I always had whatever. My mom and dad were not buying me a $600 purse."

Allowing her to get comfortable with sitting before a mirror preparing to get into the same kind of character she would years later before concerts performing in front of thousands of fans, Gaga no doubt played this role out as a teenager getting ready for school each morning where the spotlight was on her, albeit in a far different and much sadder way. Confirming that this favorite part of her morning routine cheered her up, the singer years later fondly recounted that because "I went to an all-girls school…I was very much like my mother; she would do her hair every morning and get dressed nice. So, most of the time I would stay up all night, straightening my hair, and I would even put my makeup on before bed sometimes, so that when I woke up in the morning it would be ready for school. I just liked to be glamorous. It made me feel like a star."

Working as a waitress at an Upper East Side café after class each day before coming home to practice whatever scenes for whatever play lead she was starring in at the time, the last act in a daily routine that People Magazine reported also included "working with Christina Aguilera's vocal coach, studying classical piano and singing in a classic-rock high school band at Manhattan private school Convent of the Sacred Heart."

To get a break from the stress of her daily routine, Gaga would take the money she made waitressing and disappear into downtown jazz clubs to soak up a genre that also played a major role in shaping her musical style of songwriting and performing, recalling to Larry King that "I got a job when I was 15 because my allowance was about $20 a week, which in New York was impossible. So I used to waitress across the street from where I grew up. And I used to take all the money I made waitressing so that I could go watch jazz downtown."

Looking back with pride years later on the work ethic her parents bred into her, she shard in a conversation with Larry King that "I think more than anything in my house growing up, my parents instilled a very strong work ethic in me and my sisters. So as long as I worked hard at whatever it is that I wanted to do, they were OK with me doing it. But if I was ever lazy, I would—I would reckon that they would perhaps not want me to do it." She was equally as appreciative for the high standards her school's curriculum required of her as a student during these precious formative years, telling the Guardian in 2010 that "I went to a lovely school and I got an incredible education, and I actually think that my education is what really sets me apart, 'cos I'm very smart. I don't know that my schooling was conducive to wild ideas and creativity, but it gave me discipline, drive. They taught me how to think. I really know how to think. It's like there are so many components to making a show and making art, and my school taught me how to think that way."

Describing herself as a "very dedicated, very studious, and very disciplined student," while accurate, only told one side of Gaga's real story by the time she was 17 and beginning to experiment in all sorts of things that would have surely made her parents cringe had she been less clever a rebel. Confirming in a candid moment with Vogue in 2012 that during this age "I was this really bad, rebellious misfit of a person," she dished on snippets of her highlight reel that included "sneaking out, going to clubs, drugs, alcohol, older men, younger men. You imagine it, I did it. I was just a bad kid."

By the time she was nearing graduation, her hard work was already beginning to pay off in the form of the small triumph of making her first fans locally among her fellow classmates. Winning over both previous detractors and new listeners in grades behind hers, as classmate Justin Rodriguez—who graduated with Stefani in the class of 2003—recalled to New York Magazine, by the end of their senior year, "everyone was playing her demo, like, 'Whoa, she's going to be a star. She was by far the most talented person in high school, but she'd do so many random acts of kindness, like saying, 'Your singing has gotten so much better, you're working hard and I've noticed.' She wasn't a diva at all."

"A whole project rather than just a vocalist, Lady GaGa is the determined invention of art school graduate Stefani Germanotta."

—BBC

"I was a waitress for many years. And a bartender. And I was a go-go dancer briefly as well. I used to make a lot of money to pay for demos and flyers that I used to post up all around the NYU area on the lower east side to get people to come see my shows."

—Lady Gaga to Larry King, 2010

Chapter 2

176 Stanton Street

Spinning the record backward to reveal the hidden answer to the most obvious question everyone was asking in 2009: WHERE DID LADY GAGA COME FROM??? Her rags to riches story began like many pop stars' stories do, including her most popular parallel among music critics, Madonna, who ironically like Gaga got her start in New York as an unknown starving artist/dancer-singer, and in 19-year old Stefani's case, a DJ with a WILDLY racy live act that nearly gave her father a heart attack. A period where Gaga acknowledged years later that she was willing to commit herself fearlessly to her performances to win over any audience she was playing no matter how big or small. She qualified this determination with her revelation to the Daily Mail UK that "I'd be go-go dancing in front of 15 people who didn't know who I was, but I'm a fearless person, and, as I got older, the show got more over-the-top, although I shudder now when I look back at how naive I was."

Her parents shared a similar naivety the first time they came to see their daughter's live show, causing the singer years later to shake her own head as she recounted their shocked reaction to Barbara Walters, particularly the look of horror on her father's face after he saw for the first time what had become her regular stage costume at "a club called The Bitter End (where I played)...all the time, but I had been gone for a while and it was my first time playing my new glam-inspired music, and nobody would be quiet. I walked into the room and before I even opened my mouth they were yelling and chatting and drinking and slamming their glasses, and I kept saying, 'Excuse me, hello,' and nobody would stop. So something just came over me and I took my clothes off...I left my bra and underwear on."

Though the crowds at the Bitter End were used to Gaga's revealing stage costume by the time her parents sat down to watch her perform for the first time months later, she confirmed in a memorable conversation with The Guardian in 2009 that her father—who, though stayed for the entire show—watched in shock that night as his daughter paraded around on stage in "a leopard-thong-fringed bikini with a sequined high-waisted belt and granny panties, and it was so wrong it was amazing. And he told me I did a great job, but he was shocked and alarmed. My mother told me he broke down and told her he thought I was crazy. Really crazy. Later that week my family said, 'It was just really hard to watch that show and we think you've lost your mind and we don't know what to do.'" An understandable struggle for any parent that Gaga remembered was so extreme at first that "we didn't talk for months after the first time he saw me play."

Recounting the experience from a parent's perspective, mother Cynthia shared with Oprah Winfrey years after her daughter had hit the big time that the show was indeed as theatrical and shocking as you'd expect from Lady Gaga, albeit well ahead of her arena spectacles, wherein that night "she was performing…in her bikini performing with **Lady Starlight** and decided that night to be heavy metal, to actually light hairspray on fire. And some people left when that happened and a lot of people stayed and thought it was cool, but her father and I were like, honestly he said that, 'I think she has a screw loose.'" A reflection of how much Gaga knew she had to stand out from the competition to strike a nerve, the reaction she got from her parents was, in reality, about what anyone could expect through a parent's filter, and one Stefani acknowledged was "such a drastic change from who I was in highschool, and who I became."

This was indeed a different time from the moment following the singer's graduation from high school in 2003 a few years earlier, a time when both Stefani and her parents had their expectations collectively set on high after she'd been accepted into NYU's prestigious Collaborative Arts Project 21 program. An elite and highly-competitive program, CAP21 describes itself on the official Tisch website as offering a curricula that "replenishes the American musical theatre by training the next generation of performers and infusing the entertainment industry at large with talent and source material. The goal is to create programs that achieve substantial and lasting contributions to the future of the arts…The CAP21 Conservatory provides an in-depth actor training program specializing in musical theatre performance. The school, which began in 1994, is now an internationally recognized musical theatre conservatory. Currently, through its various programs, the Conservatory annually trains 400 emerging performers who come from all over the United States and internationally. Over 100 Alumni of CAP21's Conservatory Training Programs have appeared on Broadway."

Finding herself much more at home in her new academic surroundings, Gaga recalled years later in describing what she picked up from her studies at Tisch that influenced her as a performer, she honed in on CAP21 as being "where I learned theater—I did so many shows. I would take myself on auditions and practice. Truthfully, I learned how to develop characters and communicate with the audience through monologues and really punctuated speech...I was really trying to follow their philosophy (of theatrical performers she admired like Queen and David Bowie). I started to understand how I could make music and perform in that way without being so watered down. I don't have any interest in performing in (a typical, boring way). I believe there is something in my performances that is more honest about who I am at heart."

Still, as a student, the singer admitted to feeling restless, confessing to DJ Ron Slomozicw years later that "I was kind of an asshole in school, I was the girl in class who, when the middle-aged, white male professor was giving a list of books to read and I would raise my hand and be, why aren't there any African-American writers, why isn't there anything here by anyone who's gay. I was that annoying pain-in-the-ass girl who was trying to answer every question and make the teacher look bad. It made me upset when I felt like there was a biased approach to the way I was educated." Gaga had a further communication breakdown after she faced rejection from Tisch's drama professors, recalling to Entertainment Weekly that her instructors told her at auditions: "You'll never be the heroine, the blonde, the star. Your hair's too dark. You look too ethnic."

Choosing to drop out of the program after three semesters, rather than protesting when their daughter left college or threatening to cut off financial support, as many parents would have done, the Daily Mail UK reported that, amazingly, "when she told her father of her plans for worldwide pop superstardom he used his money and connections to hire the best producers, to book studio time and to get Stefani in the room with record executives. In 2005, when she decided to drop out of NYU in her freshman year, Joe agreed to bankroll her for 12 months, paying the rent on her tiny fifth-floor walk-up on the Lower East Side and hauling her furniture up the stairs."

In a reflection of just how much Joseph Germanotta—who Gaga later called "my hero"—believed infinitely in his daughter's talent and determination, she revealed to MTV years later that her father's support was motivational mojo. Rather than discouraged by the decision to drop out, she found the experience made her feel "super-uninspired, and I just wanted to do it alone, so it was me and my piano and three jobs, and I played every club, bombed in every club, and I worked my way up." Other important motivational muses for Gaga descending directly from the artistic pool of influences she'd grown up admiring included "Queen and David Bowie, they were the key for me. When I was playing the New York rock clubs, a lot of record labels thought I was too theatrical. Then, when I auditioned for stage musicals, the producers said I was too pop…I didn't know what to do until I discovered Bowie and Queen. Their songs combined pop and theatre—and that pointed a way forward."

Taking up residence at 176 Stanton Street, the NY Daily News later reported that she "paid $1,100 for the pad, which boasts French doors, a marble bath and kitchenette," quipping years later in an article advertising the apartment for rent for $1880 that "though potential renters may not be looking for inspiration, Gaga credits living in the LES for providing her with plenty of fodder for her art." The singer painted a fuller picture of precisely what about the gritty city backdrop served as her muse, she told 60 Minutes years later that "It was like I had to go lick the ground (on the Lower East Side) for a few years to understand New York City and a whole different side of the pavement. I wanted to live alone—live in solitude with my music. I wanted to read poetry and be overly dramatic about everything and that's what I did."

Energized to finally have begun her official adventure as a starving artist, as Stefani took the step from school into the real world of introducing herself as a performer and began knocking on nightclub doors around lower Manhattan, the singer proudly reminisced years later to Vogue that her campaign to introduce herself as a solo artist was truly "grassroots, downtown New York, blood, sweat, and tears, dancing, music, whiskey, pummeling the streets, playing every venue I could get my hands on." Though the world of social media was up and running by then, Gaga still took to the old-school advertising approach of going "to Kinkos and… (getting) the expensive paper and get it laser-printed and make nice flyers, not like the ones everyone else had. And get my demo tapes copied…I was getting paid to perform so I was very excited. I was getting 400 bucks a night!"

Feeling she'd arrived at her first real place of freedom where her art could imitate life as interchangeably as her life already authentically reflected her artistic personality—from fashion to professional pursuits to the people she socialized with, without worrying about being rejected for wearing it all on her sleeve, Gaga relished the moment when she reached the realization that "I'm not really made for anything else." Confessing in the same conversation years later with Songwriter Universe that "my brain doesn't function in a way to permit me to have any other kind of life outside of music, art, fashion, and expression," the singer-songwriter revealed that she'd in fact felt this way dating back to an age so young that she didn't yet "know how to explain my passion for songwriting and performing. There was never a point where I wanted to do anything else, it's just in my blood."

Now able to wear that truth as a badge of honor as she stepped onto what would be arguably the most challenging stage she'd lived yet as a performer now that she was competing against thousands of unknown female singer-songwriter-dancers all chasing the same dream she was, rather than being intimidated, Gaga used the competition as fuel, reasoning to Elle Magazine that "as an artist, (struggle is) something I prayed for…I struggled when I was young and…(really wanted) to experience something psychotic and outer-body and magical and inconvenient to help breed my creativity, to push my tortured reality to the place of the double-rainbow."

Equally as inspired by the energy of a city whose pulse naturally moved a million miles a minute, Gaga—in her candid conversation with Vogue about the early years—readily credited "the hustle and the grind and the traffic of New York that propelled me to where I am today. I don't in any way associate my past with anything other than the hunger and the starvation for success that I still feel. It was the most beautiful time in my life." The backdrop to that beautiful time, as Vanity Fair described, centered around the "lower East Side neighborhood where she lived alone in a walk-up apartment at 176 Stanton Street from May 2005 to May 2007, after dropping out of the Tisch School of the Arts at New York University…It's where she took drugs, wrote songs, and lugged her keyboard up and down several flights of stairs to do club shows."

Pulling the curtain back on the oft-asked question of where she came up with her flamboyant stage name, arguably among the most important decisions for any unsigned recording artist looking to make a name for herself, before she graduated to Lady Gaga, Stefani revealed that "in the beginning, I used the name my parents gave me." Still 18 at the time and outset of what would become "a phase in which I ran away from myself a little," the singer hit fast-forward to a year later when "I started being called Gaga by friends when I was about 19…a bit worried about my mental health…" The beginning of a period of experimentation where the singer candidly recalled to The Guardian "I gave up my studies, tried out lots of things, including drugs…At that time I was a burlesque go-go girl in a gay bar in the Lower East Side, where I've lived since I was 18. The Lower East Side is a catchment basin for all the crazies and misfits in New York. That helped me find myself as Gaga." Tracing the name's origin even more specifically in an interview with Digital Spy to "the Queen song 'Radio Gaga,'" the singer was proud of the fact that her namesake also came as a direct reaction to her stage show, adding that "I did a lot of very theatrical performance arty shows on the Lower East Side in New York and my producer kept saying to me, 'You're so GaGa.' I was like, 'You mean like Freddie Mercury?', and decided to keep it as my name…I say to people, 'If I'm not GaGa, I really don't know who the fuck I am.'"

Exploring the implications of the name's dark side as it related to the period in her life where Gaga "ran away from myself," the measure of just how far down she'd spiraled was in fact much greater in the context of the concern even Gaga's hardest partying friends had begun to express over a casual cocaine habit that had fast become a serious addiction by the age of 19. Starting innocently enough with the seduction of the New York night club-life, Gaga would joke matter-of-factly years later that "I had enough crazy nights to last a lifetime between the ages of 18 and 21." Her spiral downward had been brought on in part by her being dropped from her first record label in 2007 in a domino effect Billboard reported began "in 2005 not long afterward, she left school so she could concentrate on her music, fronting a band called SGBand, which released two EPs prior to splitting. Germanotta then teamed with producer Rob Fusari, a collaboration that produced…recordings that led to her signing with Def Jam in the fall of 2006. Her association with Def Jam was short-lived: the label dropped her early in 2007."

Following the devastation of being dropped from her first major-label record deal, confirming years later to People Magazine that "I hit rock bottom, and it was enough to send a person over the edge," painting an even more vivid picture to Vanity Fair with her memory that as the sense of rejection set in, "I was completely mental and had just been through so much…I do not want my fans to ever emulate that or be that way. I don't want my fans to think they have to be that way to be great. It's in the past. It was a low point, and it led to disaster." The depths of that disaster translated a period of isolation where Gaga retreated inward, finding a strange comfort in what she identified to Howard Stern as "something about the drug that made me feel I had a friend. I did it all alone in my apartment, while I wrote music. And I regret every line I ever did." Aware after a while that her 'friend' had two faces, Gaga eventually hit rock bottom once she realized "it was ruining my life," adding in the same conversation with Larry King that once she woke up to the fact that it was getting in the way of her dream, "I kind of just threw it away…It's the devil."

Once her head had cleared and she began picking up the pieces in the aftermath of losing her first recording contract, a pivotal pep talk that helped get Gaga over the stigma and sting of her rejection came when she recalled to People Magazine that "my mother… (who had) screamed so loud on the other end of the phone, I'll never forget it—the day I told her about being dropped)—said, 'I'm gonna let you cry for a few more hours, and then after those few hours are up, you're gonna stop crying, you're gonna pick yourself up, you're gonna go back to New York, and you're gonna kick some ass!'"

Things soon started to turn around for starving artist Stefani once she cleaned up and met the kindred spirit who would become her on-stage soul mate, although Gaga revealed of her first time seeing Lady Starlight perform that, it wasn't in a club, but in fact go-go dancing on a bench in St. Jerome's Park! Inspiring Stefani by the plain fact that the act was just as bold and outrageous as her own in nature, the singer told Vanity Fair years later that she was drawn in to the performance piece because "there was something off about it, something awkward and uncomfortable, but she was so unapologetic and interesting; I wanted to be like that."

Hitting it off instantly once she introduced herself to Lady Starlight following the public performance, the two solo artists found they had instant chemistry, so much so that Starlight recalled in the same cover story that "we hung out, started to perform together, and people thought we were sisters, or girlfriends—neither of which we ever denied. She has such positive energy; it was so inspirational to me." Recognizing the true dimensions of Gaga's talent as a star, Gaga credited Starlight with helping her to fully define and over time refine that total package, fondly sharing her memory with Elle Magazine of the magic moment of encouragement that came when

"Starlight looked at me one day and said, "When you perform, you're just possessed. You're more than a songwriter, you're a performance artist!" Playing a critical role for helping Gaga rebuild her artistic confidence following her aforementioned crash, Starlight shined some hope back into Stephani's artistic skies "(in those early days by just trying) to show her: Don't be afraid of anything. Go to whatever lengths we need to go to to get people shocked. It was, like, live it and believe it."

She was also aided greatly by the open-minded scene she was welcomed into as a live performer, one where the LA Times later reported she got "her start in the bohemian enclaves of downtown New York City, Gaga is deeply indebted to Warhol's 'Superstar'-oriented Factory scene and its aftermath, which produced drag performers like Candy Darling, artists such as Robert Mapplethorpe and streetwise rock stars including Lou Reed and Patti Smith, who declared glamour accessible to anyone with a Polaroid camera, a glue gun or a cheap guitar."

Pooling their visions to construct a stage show starring the team of Gaga and Starlight, the resulting show would prove quite an artistic leap forward from the days "when I started out, I was pretty funky, but not quite so mad. I wore a leotard and had my hair like Amy Winehouse. I would sing and play the piano while wearing a hundred orchids in my hair. I was a real flower child, but quite sweet with it." Now a far more experienced provocateur as a performer—and working with a partner this time around—rather than working to split the risk, she and Starlight sought to push their performance to an extreme where Starlight mused to The Guardian that "we were just down to fuck with people, (had that)…punk rock mentality, just shocking people. Going to indie clubs and playing pop, and I'd spin metal in between her singing pop songs in a bikini. They hated us!"

Excited to be getting such a provocative reaction, the duo strove to push the boundaries of their show even further as they refined its outrageousness and their reputation began to spread, with Elle Magazine UK describing the resulting cabaret act as "Gaga playing synth and lighting cans of hairspray" and "Starlight playing records beneath glitter balls." Soon becoming what The New Times reported as "a popular fixture for several years in New York's club scene…(Gaga) and Lower East Side DJ Lady Starlight hosted a weekly party called 'New York Street Revival and Trash Dance' in which they performed 1970s and 1980s hits. Their outrageous performances included the lighting of cans of hair spray on fire and choreographed go-go dancing. Word got around (and before long), the two were drawing massive crowds to venues like Mercury Lounge, Bitter End, and Rockwood Music Hall."

Finally feeling like she'd made it even without having the record deal she'd once coveted, this period of first connecting with her fans on an organic, audiovisual level was vital for Gaga as she also began to experience her first true wave of not only acceptance, but actual celebrity as an artist and performer. So intensely in fact that Gaga years later in the same conversation with Elle UK confessed that "I had already thought I had made it," the singer-songwriter still drew her greatest inspiration amid all the buzz from simply seeing "all the joy and the bliss on my face and that was because I was just happy making music and happy that people were coming to see me live," including her parents.

By then, whatever concerns or objections Stefani's parents had held previously over the risks she was taking to pursue her dream, the gamble appeared to have paid off in their eyes after Gaga announced to her parents that she was moving to Los Angeles in 2007 to record a solo album, a change that motivated her father to make his peace with the past and focus on the future, which was suddenly shining very brightly for his daughter after Billboard reported that "the Lady Gaga & the Starlight Revue, a tongue-in-cheek neo-burlesque act (had) gained positive press and proved to be her last stop before signing with Interscope later in 2007."

Taking fans back to the moment of a dream coming true she'd been chasing her whole life, Lady Gaga shook her head as she recalled to Larry King that "I had moved to Los Angeles and I'd been dropped from record labels a few times, and been through so many obstacles and told no, and rejected, you're not pretty enough, can't sing enough, can't write a song good enough. You're a freak, the weird girl from New York. I mean it was a rejection after rejection. And I wrote this song 'Just Dance.' And it was my—it's my eureka moment. It was the thing that everyone was able to latch on to, the record label, the gay community who has been the most enormous blessing of my life that I have them and their support and the way that they truly understand me and support me."

Looking back on the highs and hells of the wild ride she took getting to L.A. and signing a major label deal, the singer proudly declared to Elle UK that she had no apologies for any of the past experiences that helped to mold her into the star she was about to become, "I don't regret anything. If I'd known things back then I wouldn't be where I am now, because so much of who I am is based on a lack of fear. I have no fear. It's like jumping off buildings completely blindfolded and I don't know where I'm going to land and I don't care. You have to trust the art. If you don't trust the art, it's not going to trust you to be its fuse. It's not inanimate. The art has to trust me or it's not going to invite me to be its messenger."

"In 2009 Lady Ga Ga outperformed everyone. She became the first artist ever to have 4 number one hits off her debut album."
—Barbara Walters

"I always had a lot of nerve. And insecurity."
—Lady Gaga, 2009

"I don't think I could ever be prepared for fame. I don't think that you can prepare for it or get used to it. I've felt famous my whole life, but this is a whole other level of famous."
—Lady Gaga, 2009

Chapter 3
The F.A.M.E.

Once her record deal was finally signed and Gaga had transitioned from the stage into the studio to record her debut LP, 'The FAME,' conceptually she never truly left in context of the album's thematic direction, of which MTV.com revealed heading into its August, 2008 release that "the New York-born theatrical dance-pop upstart said she didn't set out to emulate the sounds of the '70s. She just started writing music, incorporating her lifelong love of theater, fashion and pop into the material. The end result is a record that sounds like it could have come from a different period altogether." Waxing poetic on the essence of her coming vogue, Gaga explained of at the time that "it's pop, it's electronic, it's futuristic, it's fashion, it's New York, it's GaGa. I really want to make this my life and I want my work to express who I am. I want to express myself through as many mediums as possible and I want to become a master of as many artistic orifices as I can."

Delving deeper into what she felt was missing in connecting pop fans on an organic level with what they were experiencing in the surreal sense both visually and aurally as listeners that her sound/style would once again marry, the singer reasoned that "what has been lost in pop music these days is the combination of the visual and the imagery of the artist, along with the music—and both are just as important. So, even though the carefree nature of the album is something that people are latching onto right away about my stuff, I hope they will take notice of the interactive, multimedia nature of what I'm trying to do. The things I like to do and the theatrics, I like to incorporate them into the choreography. With my music, it's a party, it's a lifestyle, and it's about making the lifestyle the forefront of the music."

Gaga without a doubt would deliver the goods with the release of 'The Fame,' at least in the lofty opinions of the sort of mainstream critics that can make or break a debut artist's ambitions, no matter how grand a stand they are seeking to take, and with Gaga, they were eating it up, beginning with Billboard's declaration that "(with) her 2008 manifesto The Fame…Gaga crossed over into the mainstream, ushering out one pop epoch and kick-starting a new one, quickly making such turn-of-the-century stars as Christina Aguilera and Britney Spears seem old-fashioned, quite a trick for any artist to pull off."

Indeed, it was a rarest of feats in an age where fame hardly lasted 15 minutes anymore, and where albums hardly went platinum, the New York Times would argue that Gaga succeeded because she'd disregarded that concept entirely, "(ignoring) mid-decade trends, using an unsubtle beat, four-on-the-floor—an update of the disco thump—rather than the funk syncopations of hip-hop and R&B. Her lyrics twisted the straightforward come-ons and affirmations of most dance music; they held humor, sleaze, defiance and thoughts about ambition and celebrity."

While Gaga would become an overnight sensation in the States, her label made the smart strategic decision to debut the decade's greatest pop hope in Europe ahead of the U.S., finding the latter market far more open-minded to what the singer described as her desire to take advantage of the fact that "I think pop is ever changing, and I hope to death it never stops being so. Art is designed to be different from moment to moment, and songs should reflect that. They shouldn't all be the same. That's my ambition as an artist. I'm not particularly obsessed with how my career will be viewed when it's over. I'm much more obsessed with what I create along the way and how dedicated I am to each creation."

Embraced with open arms in Europe as she hit the road in the fall of 2008 in support of her debut LP, the BBC predicted that courtesy of "a love of synths and 80s pop, and an eye-catching image as well as an obsession with celebrity, her debut album is set to capture the heart of every pop fan as well as establishing the electro-girl revolution that looks set to conquer the close of the decade."

Her launch toward those stars would first be fueled by the momentum of FAME's debut single, 'Just Dance,' which British paper The Guardian described as "an homage to overindulgence and the restorative effects of dancing," adding that "the song is (Gaga's) opening gambit from her debut album, Fame, a ceaselessly hedonistic, sexually charged rumination on modern pop culture which sounds…(like) a blur of pop and dance and pelvic thrusting that simultaneously makes a grope in the direction of female empowerment."

As the single quickly ascended the British Pop Charts to the always-coveted peak of # 1, though confident, it was clearly not lost on Gaga how fortunate a shot at the brass ring she'd been given with the song, to the extreme that she confessed in one interview that "that record saved my life. I was in such a dark space in New

York. I was so depressed, always in a bar. I got on a plane to LA to do my music and was given one shot to write the song that would change my life and I did."

By the time it was all the radio rage across Britain, Gaga took a follow-up opportunity—now on more credibly commentary ground with a hit under her belt—to delve into what she felt within the song distinguished her from even the crème de la crème of pop peer competition, offering her opinion to that end that "it just doesn't sound like Katie Perry's "I Kissed a Girl"—which is a beautiful, lovely, amazing hit record and it sounds like a radio hit.

My song doesn't sound like a radio hit. I mean it does, but it doesn't. Now here in the UK it might, because electro-pop is not this stinky underground thing, it's a real genre. But in America electro-pop is dirty underground music." Indeed, even as Gaga's sound had found the right place to hit at the right time, back in the States, due to her genre still holding an underground status of popularity, Rolling Stone Magazine reported that, as a result, "initially Lady Gaga had greater success in Europe, thanks in large part to the 'Just Dance' single, which earned club play in the U.S. and chart placement in other territories. Gaga's march toward the top of the American chart was slow."

Nevertheless, Gaga knew with the instantly infectious British reaction to her niche brand of electro-dance pop that she was onto something as she prepared to ride the British pop invasion wave back home with a single she reasoned would eventually break just as big in the States simply because "everyone is looking for a song that really speaks to the joy in our souls and in our hearts and having a good time. It's just one of those records. It feels really good, and when you listen to it, it makes you feel good inside. It's as simple as that. I don't think it's rocket science when it comes to the heart. I think it's a heart theme song."

The song proved to have heart as 'Just Dance' fought its way for five months up the Billboard Hot 100 Singles Chart, beginning with its entry at # 76 on August 16th, 2008, and slow burn over the 6 months that followed before the single broke big, finally reaching # 2 on January 10th, 2009 with 419,000 downloads sold. After taking 26 weeks to make the climb, Gaga achieved her life-long dream of scoring a # 1 hit the following week when Just Dance topped the coveted chart position, eventually becoming only the second song in pop single history to attain the record of 6 million paid downloads.

Prior to her US success, Gaga was clearly grateful to have had her foot-in-the-door success in Britain with 'Just Dance,' commenting to that end that "it's been a long running dream to have a big hit in the UK—my fans there are so sexy and the people are so innovative and free in how they think about pop culture and music. I was in my apartment in Los Angeles getting ready to go to dance rehearsal when they called and told me, and I just cried."

By the time she was ready for the U.S., Gaga quipped that "they don't need to knock, I'm knocking down their doors," and indeed she would, but not without continuing her verbal appreciation to fans around the world for embracing 'Just Dance,' confessing in one moment of tangible honesty that "it saved my life I guess in—just as in a transitional way in terms of where I was in the journey of my music.

The single's massive success would bring Gaga another dream come true, this time from the performance side, with her opportunity to film the first of what would become a signature series of visually-dazzling music videos that helped remind music fans why video had first killed the radio star 30 years earlier.

By 2009, Gaga was seeking to re-invent both mediums in her own image, one that would raise the bar for visual value in what for years prior had been a single-driven sales model where videos played only a small part in selling an artist's brand, and 'Just Dance' provided her the perfect opportunity to get the monster ball rolling, recalling to that end of its physical shoot that "it was so fun, it was amazing.

For me it was like being on a Martin Scorsese set. I've been so low budget for so long, and to have this incredibly amazing video was really very humbling. It was really fun, but you'll see if you ever come to a video shoot of mine one day—I'm very private about those things, I don't really talk to everybody. I'm not like the party girl running around. I might even seem to be a bit of a diva. I'm sort of with myself, in my work head space worrying about costumes, and if extras look right, and placement. I don't just show up for things, you know. That video was a vision of mine. It was Molina the director who wanted to do something, to have a performance art aspect that was so pop but it was still commercial, but that felt like lifestyle. It was all those things, I love it."

In tying the sonic and theatrical components of her broader performance presentation together, Gaga reasoned that one was no less important than the other in the summary translation, explaining that "I don't write records and then decide what the video will look like. I instantaneously write things at the same time so it's a complete vision, the song and the visual, the way that I would perform it on the stage. It's something that all comes to me at once. So when I say I make the music for the dress, the dress is a bit of a metaphor for 'I make the music for everything,' for the entire performance vision."

Elaborating on why she felt this innate artistic strategy gave her an edge over her pop competition, Gaga reasoned her niche naturally stood apart from any pop peers because "its performance art. So much of what I do is way more than just the music. I design the clothing, the props, and the creative direction. For me, it's everything. I want my fans to have very specific imagery in their head when they're listening to the music. I want to hammer it into people's heads that pop music is legitimate art when it's done right. A good pop song can be played anywhere in the world for any kind of person, and it's gonna make them wanna get up and fucking dance. Like it or not, it's an incredibly powerful genre."

The potency of Gaga's message would catch on infectiously thereafter, with Rolling Stone Magazine reporting that after 'Just Dance' reached the peak position in January 2009, followed swiftly by 'Poker Face,' the single that firmly pushed her into the mainstream, its popularity growing so large it often functioned as a punch line on TV in addition to winning a Grammy for Best Dance Recording alongside nominations for earning nominations for Song of the Year and Record of the Year at the 52nd Grammy Awards, and selling 9.8 million downloads (making the single among the best-selling singles of all time). 'LoveGame' and 'Paparazzi' also appeared as singles, selling 2.5 million and 3.1 million single downloads respectively, earning Gaga her 3rd and 4th Top 10 Billboard Hot 100 Singles Chart hits, peaking at # 5 and #6 respectively.

Taking fans beyond the stage and screen and behind the scenes inside the writing and recording of 'The FAME,' beginning with the latter break-out single 'Just Dance,' Gaga took rightful credit as head visionary compositionally and for the conceptual end of her production spectrum for those songs, attesting to that end in a conversation with US Magazine that "there is not one song on any of my records that wasn't written by me, and I think when you write your own music you find ways to reinvent them emotionally through yourself." Gaga—without boasting—but rather arguably in an effort to protect herself and her art from any accusation or assumption of artificiality with her additional declaration to CNN that "I have written every single song that I have ever sang and I have also produced a lot of the music on both my records."

Still, while she was quick to plant her artistic flag in the tongue of any critic who tried to question its sovereignty, she was equally quick to throw spotlight to the album's principle producer, RedOne, who the singer-songwriter credited as creative co-pilot with being the equivalent of "the heart and soul of my universe. I met him and he completely, one hundred and fifty thousand percent wrapped his arms around my talent, and it was like we needed to work together. He has been a pioneer for the House of Gaga and his influence on me has been tremendous. I really couldn't have done it without him. He taught me in his own way—even though he's not a writer, he's a producer—he taught me how to be a better writer, because I started to think about melodies in a different way."

Clearly humbled by the success that not only 'Just Dance,' but as she caught on, the rest of his collaborative creations with Gaga had had on the collective pop public conscious, RedOne began his discussion on the making of the LP that changed pop history and brought electro-pop into the mainstream by quipping modestly that "I'm really just a guitar player. The song 'Just Dance' is really just a rock song, but we used synths instead of guitars. The drums are rock drums instead of the usual dance rhythms. When we mixed that together it created a new sound."

For Gaga, this breakthrough for pop radio was at its root possible, as the singer-songwriter explained to Vogue, because of her own native open-minded pallet of derivative inspirations, a garden of muses that married successfully with her own inspiration because "I have a very broad taste in music…(I) don't differentiate the rock star from the pop star. It's all the same thing."

Underscoring just how broadly that pallet of tastes ranged, producer RedOne recalled that during pre-production discussions prior to heading into the studio, the pair listened together to Motley Crue's "Girls Girls Girls" among other metal selections, including Iron Maiden, who Gaga revealed to Rolling Stone Magazine "changed my life…Iron Maiden has never had a hit song, but they tour stadiums around the world, and their fans live, breath, die for Maiden. That is my dream."

RedOne was so impressed by Gaga's conversational articulation of that dream and its raw musical translation as she played him rough demos back in 2008 prior to her even being signed that he recalled feeling she was worth rolling the dice on, based first and foremost on the fact that "we just connected" on a personal level. An important detail to highlight given the fact that Gaga was far from a sure-bet at a time when the producer's calendar was very much in demand based on his previous successes with artists including Akon and the New Kids on the Block's wildly successful reunion LP, The Block, which debuted at # 1 on the Billboard Top 200 Album chart at a time no one thought the band's brand had more legs than its nostalgic value.

Clearly inspired by the raw star power he saw in Gaga, in spite of the producer's revelation that "*I met GaGa before she had the deal,*" he found himself no less intrigued, continuing with his memory that "(my management) told me that she had just got dropped but that I just had to meet her. They said she was a talented writer and a beautiful artist, and I should just talk to her for five minutes to see if I wanted to work with her. So I went to the city to meet her at the Sony building. She was cool. She told me how she loved rock…played me her stuff and that got me inspired. I told her about my vision and what I thought we could do, and she loved it. We wanted to do something that was unique because I thought she was different than everybody else. It was an opportunity to do something very fresh. That day I felt like a new sound that hadn't been done before was born…*She was so open to trying new ideas. People from outer space would love GaGa…It was obvious to me that she'd have a global sound with her bridges and melodies—she writes great lyrical concepts and had a lot of drums, very rhythmic.*"

Once Gaga and her producer were in the studio with production underway, in delving into the inspiration behind the writing of what would later become the biggest pop hits of 2009, beginning with the album's lead single, 'Just Dance,' the singer summed up the song as an example of art imitating life, offering that "the whole song's about being totally wasted at a party. It's about all the things that happen when you're out and you totally lose your head. In that situation we never *really* want to stop the party so we just dance through it. You're thinking, 'Oh fuck I wanna go home!' but your friends are like, 'Don't go home you loser, have another beer', so you do, you dance and then you're fine…I was very hung-over. I wrote the song in about 10 minutes with (producer) RedOne. And it was my first time being in a Hollywood studio. Very pristine, big huge room with giant speakers."

Turning to some of the album's other autobiographical musical moments, Gaga revealed of 'Dirty Rich' that "I was doing a lot of drugs when I wrote 'Dirty Rich.' It was about two years ago, and it was about a few different things. First and foremost the record is about—whoever you are or where you live—you can self-proclaim this inner fame based on your personal style, and your opinions about art and the world, despite being conscious of it. But it's also about how on the Lower East side, there was a lot of rich kids who did drugs and said that they were poor artists, so it's also a knock at that. 'Daddy I'm so sorry, I'm so, so sorry, yes, we just like to party.' I used to hear my friends on the phone with their parents, asking for money before they would go buy drugs. So, that was an interesting time for me, but it's funny that what came out of that record—because it's about many different things—but ultimately what I want people to take from it is 'Bang-bang.' No matter who you are and where you come from, you can feel beautiful and dirty rich."

More importantly, no matter what the headspace was, Lady Gaga found music coming out of her with such constancy that she revealed to Songwriter Universe of her process that "I will just jam around in my underwear or I could be washing my dishes. I wrote the song 'Dirty Rich' and several other songs just at the piano."

Turning to the inspiration behind the wildly-popular 'Paparazzi,' Gaga shared that "the song is about a few different things—it's about my struggles, do I want fame or do I want love? It's also about wooing the paparazzi to fall in love with me. It's about the media whoring, if you will, watching ersatzes make fools of themselves to their station. It's a love song for the cameras, but it's also a love song about fame or love—can you have both, or can you only have one?"

Of the broader album, Billboard would later celebrate the consistent fact that, like the latter single, FAME was "fueled by heavy dance tracks and popping electronic beats, The Fame, the first album by the glamorous Lady Gaga, is a well-crafted sampling of feisty anti-pop in high quality. (Gaga) pulls out all the stops on The Fame, injecting hard-hitting synthesizers and crashing slicks and grooves…The Fame is in excellent standing for establishing Lady Gaga with a solid career."

Gaga would later muse that her material translated so well with fans—beginning on a lyrical level—because of the honesty she poured into her confessions, reasoning of this aspect of her authenticity as a songwriter that "unless I am both capable of and willing to reopen the wound every time I write a song, if I choose to not look inside myself to write music, I'm really not worth being called an artist at all."

In striking the masterful balance she would with FAME between promoting the message of living through your dreams even while you're still chasing them, Gaga reasoned to MTV that this concept worked because "this idea of 'the fame' runs through and through. Basically, if you have nothing—no money, no fame—you can still feel beautiful and dirty rich. It's about making choices, and having references—things you pull from your life that you believe in. It's about self-discovery and being creative. The record is slightly focused, but it's also eclectic."

Once production had wrapped on Gaga's debut LP, in articulating her strategy as a savvy pop-trends strategist for where she felt a void existed that her singularly unique sound/style had the potential to break through, the singer began by reasoning that, contrary to FAME's dance-floor driven soundscapes, "I actually wouldn't consider myself a dance artist. I think I'm bridging the gap in a few different ways, and it's mostly from a music conceptual standpoint, mixing the dance beats one second. Mixing retro dance beats with more urban melodies, and a certainly pop chorus. It's really about, in a very methodic way, almost choosing exactly what pieces of what I want to have in the record, and then watching it cross over, with my fingers crossed."

Leading up to the full album's release, the buzz building blocks having been laid with the success of 'Just Dance,' critics like the Houston Chronicle were already beginning to throw respect Gaga's way, courtesy in the latter paper's case of the observation that "Lady GaGa, if nothing else, deserves *some* credit for bringing real dance music to the masses. Her tunes have popped up for months on *Dirty Sexy Money*, the *Miss Universe* pageant, *So You Think You Can Dance* and *Gossip Girl*."

Though the strategy took time to erupt, with MTV reporting that The FAME, initially released on August 19th, 2008, "to little fanfare (it sold just 24,000 copies in its first week here in the States)…slowly began to burrow itself into the public consciousness, thanks to an unending stream of singles—'Just Dance,' 'Poker Face,' 'LoveGame,' 'Paparazzi'—artistic videos and ambitious, eye-popping live shows. What started as a well-kept secret eventually became a worldwide phenomenon, as her singles went to the tops of charts around the globe, and The Fame moved more than 8 million copies."

In musing on why her fire took as long as it did to catch on for as big as it would go on to be, Gaga reasoned that a slow burn began when "the fashion community in general got me much earlier than everyone else. But actually, I felt truly embraced by this London cultural movement, that McQueen, Isabella, Daphne Guinness wing of the English crowd. I remember when I first started doing photo shoots, people would say, 'My God, you look so much like Isabella Blow, it scares me.' And McQueen used to say, 'Oh, my God, your boobs!' He actually grabbed both of them and said, 'Even your boobs are like hers!'"

While Gaga's style would prove a great advertisement for her brand, it was her music which ultimately drew an army of fans, even as her presence on pop radio had a gradual climb to the top of the charts, her producer RedOne reasoned this "songs like 'Just Dance' and 'Poker Face' got resistance from radio at first because they were so different. But once they got an opening and radio stations started playing those songs everybody wanted that sound. It's an incredible feeling."

The BBC would recognize the producer's key to opening ears to Gaga's sound with their nod in a review of F.A.M.E. to the "consistent production from the Red One." It would be MTV who made the connection between the album's production and how it led not only to chart success for Lady Gaga, but equally as importantly in establishing her credibility as a legitimate recording artist vs. a passing fad, by noting that the "slickly produced, genre-mashing, joy-inducing pop/dance bonanza…(landed Gaga) five Grammy nominations, including a nod for Album of the Year."

Welcoming the celebrity she'd craved her whole life and clawed her way to the top of the charts to get, once Gaga had successfully made the transition from Lower Manhattan topless club stages to headlining arena gigs around the world, she remained appropriately humbled by her fans' worldwide embrace, confessing to Interview Magazine that "its been a life-changing year for me creatively as a musician and a performance artist. I walk away from the Fame Ball humbled by my little monsters-my fans-and proud of the Haus for all its successes amidst the adversity of the industry. We killed it."

As ambitious as ever to hold on to stardom now that she'd finally ascended to the place of recognition she'd been trying to reach her whole life, Gaga expressed an impressive realism in her perspective on how long she had yet to go to truly reach the comparative heights of superstars like Madonna critics loved to compare her to, reasoning in a candid conversation with the Guardian in the wake of her wild success with F.A.M.E. that "I guess success is only as big or small as you see it. I thought I was quite successful two years ago, and I think I'm quite successful now, but I've got a long way to go. It's funny, I was sitting in the car and my manager's reading me off all the stats and the things that are happening, and he's like, 'This is great GaGa!' And I'm like, 'I know, but for some reason I feel like we've accomplished nothing and we've got so far to go.' And he's like, 'You're on the same page as me.' You know what I mean?"

"I'd rather be critically acclaimed by my fans."
—Lady Gaga, 2011

"I didn't used to be brave, but you have made me brave, little monsters."
—Lady Gaga, 2010

Chapter 4
Little Monsters

As Lady Gaga fever spread around the globe, at first it wasn't radio's wave she rode, but rather word-of-mouth raves about not only her music but her message, one that throughout her 2009 world-tour promoting only her FIRST studio LP, 'FAME,' soon amassed an army of rabidly devoted fans that Gaga affectionately named her 'Little Monsters,' explaining on the Larry King Show in 2010 with an almost paternal affection that "when I went on tour, my fans were so—they were salivating at the mouth and they couldn't—they were rabid. They couldn't wait for me to sing my new songs, and they just behaved like monsters…in the audience. So a couple of nights I just said you little monsters. I had used the lyric on the album as well, little monsters. So I just started calling them my little monsters, and before I knew it, they were all holding their hands up like this in the audience. And then this became the symbol for the little monster. And now they stand—they stand in the audience every night and they dance and they hold up their monster hands."

Much like Jay Z's live fan base loyally flashing their own diamond symbol or Ozzy Osbourne's fans raising their traditional metal horn hand gesture, for Gaga and her 'Little Monsters,' their symbology was instantly as sacred a band of the hand—one whose connection between artist and audience was so fervid that The Guardian UK in a 2010 live concert review in Britain underscored the intensity of the connection by noting that "(Gaga) is the biggest pop star in the world, who doesn't have fans so much as disciples." In a reciprocal declaration of devotion, Gaga had shared a year earlier in 2009 regarding the intensity of her dedication to her fans that "I live and create only for them."

With commercial considerations taking enough care of themselves to afford her such freedom from concern over trying to appeal to any other demographic than those listeners she desired to market herself to, thankfully for Gaga, with a universally-appealing message of acceptance, Time Out London recently noted that "no megastar in history has been able to connect with their audience so easily."

Akin to a group of former outcasts finally finding a social clique where they could fit in by just being themselves, as Gaga established her brand of POP-ularity in her own terms and on a universal turf where everyone was welcome to the party, the work-a-holic superstar was smart enough to know that owning the brand universal meant her brand had to stay open 24 hours a day, reasoning in a conversation with Elle to that end that "I think about them all the time, they wanted somewhere to go and someone to know, where they could escape from the reality of their own trauma and know we could tell the lie of surrealism over and over until it came true."

While that surrealism involved a genuine escape from the sort of brutal rejection Gaga herself had suffered growing up, she and her fellow victims of such torturous social dejection wore their scars proudly as survivors, with Gaga qualifying this connection by suggesting that "if you were not bullied in high school I can imagine that it might be a bit difficult to be around us, because we kind of flock together. But there's no discrimination. I mean if you were a cool kid at school, that doesn't mean you're not welcome. I'm not trying to further divisiveness. Those people who feel bullied or like nerds, I'm trying to make them feel like winners, but I'm not trying to make them hate all of the cool kids more. It's all about closing the gap and bringing people closer together. And that's what the pop end of my music is all about."

Likening her records and live shows to a home where she kept an almost paternalistic watch over her millions of devoted fans, Gaga revealed that she related to her fans closely enough to consider them her extended family, sharing therein that "the *love I feel for my fans, the love that they've given to me. That is like—it's so precious—you can't even imagine it. I must sound like when women give birth; they say you can't imagine how you feel until you give birth. Its how I feel. It's so funny, this morning one of my fans got my phone number. They were so sweet, they sent me a photo of them with these masks on, they were going to a 21st birthday. They were calling and texting and telling me how much I inspire them. I started to respond and talk to them because I felt so bad, I didn't want to ignore them, I knew they knew it was me. I just told them how much I loved them. They were like: 'We love you mother monster, we're wearing these masks because we love you, you've changed our lives, we can be ourselves.' I was in bed crying because I loved them so much. They were sending me these sweet little photos, I was scolding them to be safe and not drink too much even though it was their 21st birthday. I would say most of my fans are quite troubled. I look into the audience and it's like tiny little mirrors—they remind me of myself. So many of them are insecure, hate their parents, don't fit in at school, are cutters or have depression. Some of them are nine and just like pop music, some are 35 and are on a night out with the boys—it varies. I'd say there's a vast majority of them that are troubled, want to fit in and feel like freaks. They want to go out, raise their freak flag high above their head and be freed. The show is a free place for them. I created the show for my fans to have a place to go—a safe place, an electric chapel. It's their hat—their social canopy.*"

While she sought with the aforementioned social canopy to provide a refuge of sorts for her fans, in the same time, as any good parent figure would, she didn't shelter them from the truth, offering to that end in 2010 that "I always try to be honest with my fans, because I feel like I've built this goodwill with them where they know that I'm telling them the truth."

By 2009, only a year into her star's rapidly rising climb up the charts, critics finally began catching onto a buzz that had been building among fans around the world for months following the release of her debut LP, one that Interview Magazine captured poignantly in their observation that same year that "the Gaga epidemic has clearly gone global," with Elle Magazine offering a more substantive conclusion that "the mass audience is responding to the clothes show, the pounding R&B and the soap opera of her media presence, but the hardcore fans—the 'little monsters, the underdogs of love'—have dug deep inside her cartoon world to locate some common ground."

Clearly feeling the authentic connection between she and her fans was life imitating art and vise versa, Gaga explained to Vogue she felt the kindred nature of her relationship with her fans was a reflection of the fact that "I see myself in them…I look at them, and every show there's a little more eyeliner, a little more freedom, and a little more 'I don't give a fuck about the bullies at my school.' For some reason, the fans didn't become more Top 40. They become even more of this cult following. It's very strange and exciting."

Elaborating on the intensity of the seemingly-kinetic and electric connection the singer described sparking between she and her audiences at live shows, Gaga confessed in the same conversation that "sometimes, being onstage is like having sex with my fans. They're the only people on the planet who in an instant can make me just lose it."

Seeking in those moments—and in her music more generally—to take that emotion to its extreme, Gaga offered to Barbara Walters that ultimately, with every such intimate interface, "I wanna liberate them—I wanna free them of their—of their fears—and make them feel that they can create their own space in the world." Fleshing out that ambition with a multi-colored collage of fans that the LA Times reported in the context of her self-proclaimed 'Little Monsters' was "one formed by her core fan base, a mix of gay men, bohemian kids and young women attracted by Gaga's style and her singable melodies."

Regardless of their eclectic makeup, one universal ground-rule of understanding between Gaga and her fans—amounting to a very real credo—was that of universal acceptance, beginning for the singer with the key fact that "my fans don't care what I am, that's what I like about them. They don't care if I'm a boy or a girl or an in-between or a phoenix or a mermaid or a unicorn, or if I have hair one day and no hair the next. They don't care. What I love about ambiguity and irony is that it always leaves big gaping questions."

One message Gaga sought to convey consistently to her 10 million Twitter followers was that regardless of who she sought to portray or represent in character terms on stage or record, where the real-life translations of those caricatures came to life for her fans, it was clearly important to Gaga that they practiced what her message preached, such that "in terms of education—sexual education, political education and social education schools—I think it's important to be specific about civil rights and a person's worth. No person is worth any less than another human being based on their sexual orientation or religion. My admiration for the gay community comes from an incredibly steadfast and joyful courage and very bravery that they have for one another, for their community. To—to be gay and to live openly in this society is something that requires a tremendous amount of strength and steadfastness. And I admire that. And I envy it in so many ways, because it is something that I, as a woman, do not always wholeheartedly possess. And I think that my connection to them has actually been just symbiotic and mutual. They—they know how much I love them. And my music in so many ways—my friends since I was very young were all gay. And they were always my closest friends, my purest friendships. Gay men never wanted anything from me but my life and my friendship. It was—it's—it's very different than the relationships with straight men. So I suppose it's just very pure. And I celebrate their culture and their—their union and who they are, through in through, in my music, and in my fashion, and in my work, every day. And I will forever."

Turning to the question of how she handled her own face-to-face interactions with fans, while she traveled with a round-the-clock security detail, Gaga offered that such measures were purely precautionary because "*I would say ninety nine point nine infinity percent of the time, I'm not afraid of my monsters. Every once in a while there is perhaps an extra troubled fan that really wants to see me or speak to me. I'm always quite funny because my security go crazy and freak out, I'm like: 'It's okay, they're rad, they just need someone to talk to.' I've actually been in situations before like that where I've contacted parents and told them I think their little monster needed some help, attention and love. So no, I'm not afraid. One time someone came on stage and I don't know how they got on stage. I got scared for a second—you never really know, people take drugs and are having a good time at the show. I'm never really scared, just surprised. I wouldn't say I'm very often scared, more surprised and concerned. I just want to help them. I talk to my fans all the time, so no, I'd say I'm certainly never scared.*"

Seeking unlike most of her rare club of pop peers who preferred when off stage to be removed from the limelight—including not just the paparazzi but often by default direct, unfiltered contact with their fans as well—Gaga opted to employ an opposing approach of remaining approachable no matter how her fame continued to swell and create the potential for such a bubble to form. Explaining she felt this accessibility with her fans on both artistic and personal levels was necessary because "*we have a special and honest relationship,*" one that Gaga confessed was at times as much a *form of therapy for her as her music was for fans in their own everyday lives.* Elaborating on that reciprocal relationship in action, the singer began by volunteering that *"it's almost comical to talk about because I go on stage sometimes and I've had a really bad day or something's wrong. The other day I revealed to my fans that my Grandpa's sick and he's in the hospital. It's difficult for me, I'm away but I want to be home but I don't want to disappoint my fans. They spend all their money on tickets. I sat down at the piano and said to them I had a bad day my Grandpa is sick. The next day I went to, as usual, say hello to my fans on Twitter, let them know what I've been doing. I saw all these lovely messages and worldwide they trended 'get well Grandpa Gaga.' That has nothing to do with my music, my clothes or making an album number one—that's just pure friendship. The new album that I'm creating, which is pretty much finished, was written with this instinctual energy I've developed getting to know my fans. They protect me so now it's my destiny to protect them."*

Where her fans did show love to Gaga in the form of personalized mementous and tributes of a similar varietal, she appeared genuinely flattered by and grateful for the love shown her in a dream come true from the rejection and isolation she'd experienced growing up, dreaming of the kind of embrace that had finally come true with her stardom, commenting to that end that *"I feel so blessed. It's so unexplainable; the love I feel for my fans, how they treat me, all the videos they create, the lovely notes and artwork. Just the other day I spent hours reading all this fan mail sent to me, sending back autographs and looking at artwork. I sat with Haus of Gaga and people I work with on the crew and we all raved about how talented and lovely my fans are. All I can say is love is a symbiotic thing: especially when it's real. Perhaps it's just very real. I put love into my fans and they put love into me: we continue to give love back forth to each other, forever."*

The main portal through which Gaga stayed so intimately and instantly connected came courtesy of the social media revolution, telling SHOWStudio.com in 2010 that *"I actually think part of why Twitter is so great is because, for me, you can build trust with your fans—if you use it for the right reasons. People that argue on Twitter or are just using it as a celebrity networking device—it's boring and has nothing to do with your fans or your vocational purpose. I use the Internet—I've embraced the Internet in a pop cultural kind of way. I think about what a pop artist would have done in the 70's or 80's if the Iinternet was as it is today. Warhol would have done something beyond what I do and what we all do with the Internet because it's so powerful and it can reach so many people. Even previewing music videos and things: I can use the television but the truth is that the Internet is more powerful because it gives other people the platform to have a voice: you can comment, you can chat, you can make friends (safely.) I guess my point is I think it's wonderful to embrace that there are now two windows. I just embrace the Internet. Its what a pop artist should do, it's the new era, it's the way we live. We are wired."*

Beyond the real-life confidence, Gaga also drew an artistic confidence and inspiration from her fans real-life acts of devotion, reflected in her songwriting on the level that the singer confessed in 2011 that "I would say my biggest inspiration is my fans. I feel like they subconsciously submit all of their freedom, their love and their joy into me through the show and through my communication with them. It's almost like we have our own little spiritual connection that's completely separate from anything else."

In summing up what she ultimately desired to give back to her fans through the gift of her music, Gaga clearly desired to inspire *"them to love themselves. If I could, for a moment, just inspire you to love yourself—that would be worth everything." In this spirit, as she looked toward the release of her next studio LP, 'Born this Way' heading into 2011 and beyond in typically-visionary fashion, Gaga reasoned* that "because as an artist and as a performer, the person that they look up to to create this space of freedom and escapism, I want to give my fans nothing less than the greatest album of the decade. I don't want to give them something trendy. I want to give them the future."

"I had this dream and I really wanted to be a star and I was almost a monster in the way that I was fearless with my ambitions."

—Lady Gaga to Barbara Walters

Chapter 5

The F.A.M.E. Monster E.P.

Even after her F.A.M.E. LP moved 4,525,000 copies at retail, Gaga's fans wanted more, and Gaga was eager to give it to them, resulting 'The F.A.M.E. Monster EP,' not just a filler leftovers offering of songs left on the cutting room floor, but rather a collection of songs credible enough with her fan-base to take on a life of their own at retail and radio, as the LA Times attested in their thumbs-up review that "Lady Gaga lives by the credo of 'Go big or go home'—that goes for her wardrobe, her choruses and her sexual innuendo. So it makes sense that in an age of skimpy cash-grab reissues, Gaga would buck the system with 'The Fame Monster,' a deluxe version of her 2008 debut that comes equipped with eight new tracks. The New York dance-pop diva is even selling the extra tunes as a standalone EP to avoid ripping off early adopters; by major-label standards, that's more value than you shake a disco stick at." Billboard admiringly added in their glowing review of the LP that "as if Lady Gaga's debut album, 'The Fame,' wasn't loaded with enough hits-four No. 1s on Billboard's Mainstream Top 40 chart, to be exact-the set's companion EP boasts eight new tracks, nearly all of which are worthy of heavy rotation."

Reflecting the demand for her product at retail and on the streets in the bootleg market—a consequence of the buzz on the street about Gaga that was making her the hottest retail commodity all around, confidently confessing to Billboard at the time that "we always just assumed we were going to sell records. I have a sense of optimism and liberation, despite the state of the industry and the economy. We function like the industry is in full bloom, and that audacity works for us."

Using the opportunity to play a game of creative clean-up on her new favorite topic, Gaga explained to Yahoo Finance that "on my re-release The Fame Monster, I wrote about everything I didn't write on The Fame. While traveling the world for two years, I've encountered several monsters, each represented by a different song on the new record: my 'Fear of Sex Monster,' my 'Fear of Alcohol Monster,' my 'Fear of Love Monster,' my 'Fear of Death Monster,' my 'Fear of Loneliness Monster,' etc. I spent a lot of nights in Eastern Europe, and this album is a pop experimentation with industrial/Goth beats, 90's dance melodies, an obsession with the lyrical genius of 80's melancholic pop, and the runway. I wrote while watching muted fashion shows and I am compelled to say my music was scored for them. I also composed a ballad for the album, 'Speechless,' a song for my father, and it's my favorite work of all. I wrote every piece on the road—no songs about money, no songs about fame. I wrote it for my fans, so I wrote everything in between."

Shaking her head for as sure as she sounded about the flight to stardom she was piloting, the singer revealed on the human side to Vogue that "my ride through the industry was an interesting one because people loved me but there was a very big raised eyebrow about me. I mean, a big one. So people were kind of like, well, I'm involved but not really. And as soon as I took off, it was like,

The F.A.M.E. Monster E.P.

I invented her, I made her, I wrote the music. When, in reality, I am completely self-invented."

Conceptually, at heart, The Fame Monster E.P. was a mini-documentary of FAME itself, examining its all-consuming nature, one that the singer reasoned in a discussion with Larry King had taken on a life unto itself since her phenomenon had begun, an experience Gaga explained inspired a creative headspace where "I wrote the album 'The Fame Monster' which is the second album. And when I had finished, I realized that I had written each song about a particular fear that I had come across on my journey promoting the fame." Still, while Gaga was proving a born-saleswoman of her brand by marrying herself as a star to the keyword FAME, for as bright as her 24-hour-a-day life in the limelight seem in surface conversation, deeper within the album's narrative were confessions of an isolating loneliness that seemed at times to paint Gaga as a prisoner of her own device, confessing in a conversation with the Scottish Daily Record & Sunday that "the new songs are about the dark side of fame. They deal with the fact it's now impossible for me to go out without being recognized. The desire for fame knows no limits and this fascinates me. There are people who even commit murder just to become a celebrity."

True to her promise to stay as naked and transparent with her fans at all times no matter what costume she was wearing on the video screen or concert stage, in delving deeper beneath her professional surface into the personal highs and hells of life in the fast lane, Gaga explained that while "I enjoy my work…there are times when I would gladly be anonymous. I can't even drive a car. I don't have a driver's license. I have a rented apartment in New York. That's it. When I travel I have almost all of my possessions with me. That's how little I own. But my life has changed completely. The only thing that hasn't changed is my ambition. That means it's become even bigger, because I consider my music to be very important and relevant. There could be the upbringing label I'm devoting myself to art more than ever because I lead such a lonely life."

Discussing the impact of her fame on her family and their relationship with each other, Gaga revealed in the same conversation that *"I was slightly insensitive at first. I had arguments with my parents and I said: 'You guys gotta get it together, you have to stop freaking.' It was hard for everyone: I don't want my parents or friends to be incessantly asked about me, or: 'Can you ask her to do this?' It's difficult on friends and family but we made it through. I think part of making it through is that I started to grow up a little bit and, for myself, be able to understand how my career has affected the people that I love. I've been able to be more open about it, which I wasn't able to do before. To be quite frank, I still have no fucking clue how people perceive me. Sometimes my mom tries to explain it to me and I'm like 'Mom, what are you trying to say?' I think in another way, my friends and family love that about me. I'm very much just an Italian girl from New York that's got a lot of light on her face and is trying to follow the spotlight but doesn't know what's going on. I'm very naive in that way. It's okay now, everyone's good. I haven't really lost anyone—a few—but the real people you love, they're there."*

Opening up even more candidly on the costs of fame, in contrast to the visual impression her videos portray of a 24-hour party, Gaga shared of the dark side of fame in that "when you're on tour you're rather insulated from life. You are totally focused on your performances and don't really notice much else. You spend a lot more time in hotel rooms than people might think. On those nights I often sit up and compose so that I can remain in contact with my creative core. People assume that when I'm off stage I transform back into someone else. But I truly believe in the glamorous lifestyle that I present to the outside world. I love glamour. A glamorous life is quite different to a life of luxury. I don't need luxury. For years I was practically broke but I was still vain and glamorous. I don't send assistants running around to get me the perfect latte. I'm not a conceited diva. I just tend to work to the point of exhaustion and maybe demand a little too much of the people who deal with me every day."

The demands of her professional world took a toll on her romantic life as well, so much so that the singer confessed to Vanity Fair that, due to the constant devotion and dedication her professional life required, "I'm perpetually lonely. I'm lonely when I'm in relationships. It's my condition as an artist…I'm drawn to bad romances. And my song ('Bad Romance') is about whether I go after those [sort of relationships] or if they find me. I'm quite celibate now; I don't really get time to meet anyone." Looking at this as the same price that any number of superstars she'd admired while fighting to get to this point had to pay in their own right, Gaga reasoned that it was inevitable "in order for me to be successful," adding in the same conversation with Time Out London in 2011 that "in order to be a great artist—musician, actor, painter, whatever—you must be able to be private in public at all times. That is what we do."

Seeking to squeeze the most out of the premium she was paying personally for her professional success, Gaga used the sacrifice as muse, resulting in a stylistic musical montage that the LA Times revealed "includes the turbocharged Euro-soul of lead single 'Bad Romance,' the bubbly, ABBA-style pop of 'Alejandro' and 'Speechless,' and a sweeping glam-rock number seemingly modeled after David Bowie's 'Ziggy Stardust' phase. In 'Telephone,' Gaga is joined by Beyoncé for a carefully considered meditation on how annoying it is when a dude keeps calling you while you're throwing down at the club. And 'Teeth,' the EP's closer, is a sassed-out R&B jam produced by new jack swing pioneer Teddy Riley; like Gaga's piano-bar rendition of her own 'Poker Face,' it emphasizes the no-frills vocal talent beneath the art-directed glitter…The New York dance-pop diva is even selling the extra tunes as a standalone EP to avoid ripping off early adopters; by major-label standards, that's more value than you shake a disco stick."

Coinciding with the "Cha-ching!" of cash registers opening at Christmas season all over the country, Rolling Stone Magazine later would report that "Gaga released The Fame Monster in time for the holiday season of 2009. The mini-LP, available separately and as a package with The Fame, contained the single 'Bad Romance' whose popularity soon rivaled 'Poker Face' and helped kickstart a stellar year for Gaga in 2010. That year, the hit singles 'Bad Romance,' 'Alejandro,' and the Beyoncé duet 'Telephone,' along with the successful Monster Ball Tour, put Lady Gaga front and center with the public." Certified Platinum by the end of the year after debuting at # 5 (selling 151,000 units in its first week) on the Billboard Top 200 Album Chart, the E.P. would wind up becoming the dark horse winner at the 53rd Grammy Awards the next spring in 2010. Validating once and for all the fact that the new collection of songs was far from merely a vanity release without artistic substance, The F.A.M.E. Monster E.P. went on to earn a coveted nomination for 'Album of the Year,' and won for 'Best Pop Vocal Album,' 'Best Female Pop Vocal Performance' ('Bad Romance'), while 'Telephone' was nominated for 'Best Pop Collaboration with Vocals' and 'Dance in the Dark' picked up a nomination for 'Best Dance Recording.'

Clearly proud of the fact that she had turned "all the positive things you can use about fame into great things," Gaga reasoned in an interview with Vogue in 2012 that fame "will only change you and affect you if you allow it to," adding that "you have to reject all the evils of it," a strategy she had clearly mastered 2 short years into a career where Billboard noted that "even as she's becoming omnipresent, with her songs mingling with those who co-opt her on the radio, she is still slightly skewed, willing to go so far over the top she goes beyond camp, yet still channeling it through songs that are written, not just hooks. The Fame Monster builds upon those strengths exhibited on The Fame, offering a credible expansion of the debut and suggesting she's not just a fleeting pop phenomenon."

With the lines so happily blurred between life imitating art and visa verse, Gaga was living her fame 24 hours a day without taking every breaking character, telling SHOWStudio.com that she was so much as Lady Gaga that "*I sleep in all my glamorous glory. It's*

The F.A.M.E. Monster E.P.

very funny: Jimmy Iovine, who is the president of Interscope records: we took a flight together from Heathrow to L.A. and he was pissing himself laughing because he could not understand how I was watching a movie for like 12 hours straight, drinking out of my tea cup, full make-up, outfit and hair done. He was laughing so hard, he couldn't understand. He said I reminded him of Stevie Nicks. I can't help how I am, I'm a Lady. I don't want to be seen in a Virgin Mobile sweat suit." Ultimately, the thing that kept Gaga's feet on the ground even as her career continued skyward, she told Larry King in 2010, was her love affair NOT with fame itself, but rather with those responsible for her having any in the first place, explaining that "I enjoy my fans. My fans are something I could never trade or even dream of giving up. But there are many things that come with it that I perhaps do not enjoy. You know, at the end of the day, I would much rather not go to the Hollywood party. I would much rather go to the pub around the corner and buy everyone a drink."

Lady GaGa—Career on the Rise

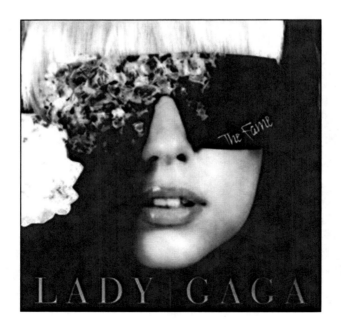

Lady Gaga with Akon

Akon, Doug Morris, Lady Gaga and Jimmy Iovine share a moment

Lady Gaga: Born to be Free

Lady Gaga in the spotlight

Lady Gaga the crowd pleaser

Lady GaGa—Career on the Rise

Lady Gaga—strong & sexy

Lady Gaga as the Fame Monster on the LP "ad Romance" - Its lead single, "Bad Romance", was a commercial success, topping the charts in more than twenty countries worldwide, while reaching number two on the Billboard Hot 100 in the United States. (Released October 26, 2009 on Interscope Records)

Lady Gaga incognito with her Former Manager Troy Carter

Lady Gaga on the red carpet with her Former Manager Troy Carter

Lady GaGa—Career on the Rise

Lady Gaga's meat dress was by far the most outrageous fashion moment of the 2010 Video Music Awards last night. It was her third and final outfit change of the night (she wore it to accept her Moonman for Video Of The Year).

Lady Gaga poses with her choreographer Richy Jackson at the 2013 MTV Video Music Awards in Brooklyn, New York.

Lady Gaga: Born to be Free

Lady Gaga poses with Miss Piggy and Kermit

Lady Gaga gets her hair together with soda can rollers

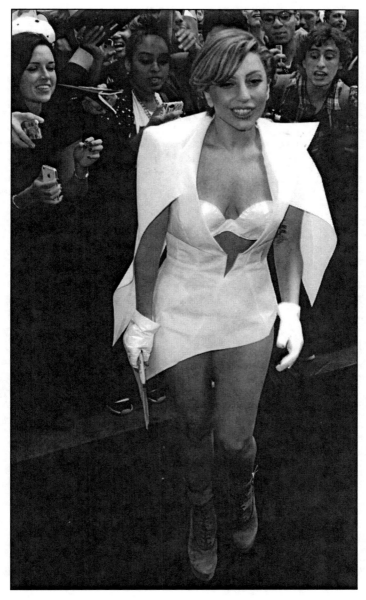

Lady Gaga makes a grand entrance, cheered on by adoring fans

Lady Gaga: Born to be Free

"It's always very strange when people say, 'Is this the real you?,' or 'Is this really who you are? Is this an act?' 'Born This Way' is sort of the answer to all of the questions I've been asked for the last three years. This is who I am."

—Lady Gaga, May, 2011

"Once an artist's biggest source of income, recorded music now plays second fiddle to touring, endorsements, merchandise sales and an array of other revenue streams once considered ancillary. That's especially true for an artist like Lady Gaga, who has lined up more branding and promotional deals in the last six months than most artists will in a lifetime."

—New York Times, 2011

"Maybe I'm out of my mind, but I believe the number of albums we're going to sell is ridiculous."

—Lady Gaga

Chapter 6

Born This Way

Freedom of expression has long been a cliché thrown around in pop music by artists who more often than not in the past decade have been too afraid to truly take the kind of chances in exercising their freedom to push stylistic boundaries that are required to redraw them at all, let alone in or on one's own terms. With the release of her sophomore LP, 'Born this Way,' Lady Gaga would become the Millennium's first true rebel leader, breaking free from the chains of conformity by turning both eyes and ears on in the same time to a new musical manifesto that preached what the singer-songwriter revealed was a message rooted in "the idea (that)…you are your image, you are who you see yourself to be. It's iconography. Warhol and I both went to church when we were younger. That's how I see things. I don't want anyone to feel trapped by their own lives. That to me is more dangerous than anything."

Giving her fans permission to believe in themselves as confidently as she did herself was an authority she would reason she'd earned "based on so many years of rejection, so many years of being told no. I internalized that rejection and turned it into something positive. I said, 'I can do this. I can be greater. I know I have what it takes.'" As she suited up ahead of the album's release to become what Rolling Stone Magazine would later (describe as) "the perfect vessel for a broad message of unity, defiant self-respect and personal liberty, themes that the pop star returns to over and over again on "Born This Way," Gaga elaborated in that spirit that "the album is about rebirth in every sense. It's about being able to be reborn over and over again until you find the identity inside of yourself that defines you best for who you are, that makes you feel the most like a champion of life."

Feeling this responsibility not only to herself as a recording artist, but perhaps even more profoundly to her listeners based on the belief that she was arguably the one role model who related authentically enough to her young fans to have an authentic shot at breaking through enough of the traditionally-out-of-reach social and generational barriers to inspire hope in a real, tangible way, Gaga offered toward that end that *"with my next album, I'm much more aware of my spiritual connection with my little monsters: every artist is a leader in that way. I don't particularly think that sex and drugs and talking about things in that way are wrong or bad for kids, I just think the most terrible thing you can do is be prejudiced. I would say that, emphatically in my career, I am VERY against prejudice and judging any particular kind of people or idea. I think it's important to be free and full of non-judgment—that is how I religiously and spiritually lead my fans in that way. I'm okay with that responsibility. I wasn't always aware of it—I'm aware that within my work sometimes I don't think about it: in my music, videos or lyrics. There is also personal expression. I have to show how I really feel about things, I can't only think about doing what's wrong or right—it's so religious. I think religion is completely bogus. I believe in God, I'm a very religious person—but religion is quite bogus. Religion does hate one kind of person. I struggle with it, I don't know if someone would be offended by me saying religion is bogus, I feel I have a good opinion about how young people are taught and how we are mind controlled into seeing things a certain way. I think the most important thing to learn is to love and be non-prejudiced."*

As its official release date approached in late May, 2011, the buzz surrounding 'Born this Way' was in essence the equivalent of Madonna's 'Like a Virgin,' a declaration of pop war on all things that had bent or bowed to trends Gaga was looking to reinvent entirely in precisely the derivative spirit Madonna had a quarter-century before with a cosmic chart-topping debut that impressed the New York Times to argue in their review of the album that "no phenomenon illustrates more pointedly how pop music history seems to run in cycles than the overnight success of the 24-year-old pop siren known as Madonna." This comparison was further substantiated—the paper would further muse—by the millions of "teen-agers…lining up in stores to purchase the album the way their parents had lined up to buy the Beatles records in the late 60's." Though iPods may have been the preferred purchasing platform by 2010, as Lady Gaga prepared to become the Material Girl's first legitimate Millennium heir apparent after drawing not just critical comparisons, but commercial proof in the form of upward of the 1.1 million copies of 'Born this Way' sold in its first SEVEN DAYS of release. Commenting on the Madonna comparisons, while it was clear Gaga was flattered by the parallel, she was equally eager to strike her own gold as the touchstone popstar for her own generation, telling FT Magazine in 2011 that "she's wonderful and inspiring and liberating, and she's certainly inspired my album, as did David Bowie, as did Prince, as did Michael Jackson, as did Grace Jones, and I would never take that away. So there's my mission statement, is if anything, thank you from the bottom of my heart for comparing me to these legendary people."

Quickly proving she was not just record making but record breaking, it was within the wake of Gaga's whiplash success that came the inevitable 'How did She Do That?' muse on the part of both curious critics and an ever-struggling record industry, whose collective attention Gaga had commanded after pulling off a feat so rare in the modern day of record sales. The historical significance of the achievement was not lost for a moment on the savvy star, who sought to tie the song's transcendent success to something greater than the latest 15-minute trend, reasoning in an interview that "I'm quite pleased with the way that it's all panned out because I knew that the first single would benefit from whatever hype, the excitement of the album coming out, and I said to myself, 'Well, let's not waste all that hype with some dingy shallow message. Let's put something really special, really powerful and beautiful, something about equality, something about freedom, something about being proud of who you are.' And what's been so nice is not only to watch 'Born This Way' be like… it was the fastest selling digital song in history, but to see it linger. It sort of like goes up and down the charts like a seesaw and it just won't go away. It's so sweet."

Her handlers were clearly pleased as well, beginning with Vice Chairman of Interscope Geffen A&M Records Steve Berman's revelation that leading up to the release of 'Born this Way,' "we wanted to approach this like we were opening a blockbuster film. It became: 'We'll put a flag in that date well in advance. We won't move. And what we'll do for the next six months is pour gas on that fire every day, really branding the date.'" Qualifying just how big an event they felt the release of Gaga's break-out album would be, the New York Times reported in 2011 that "like any good movie campaign the selling of 'Born This Way' began nearly a year in advance and continued as a well-timed drumbeat of promotional appearances, retail tie-ins and media deals that rose to a climax as the release date approached. Lady Gaga announced the title of the album at MTV's Video Music Awards last September and gave the release date on New Year's Eve. As the promotions piled up in recent weeks, she became inescapable. If you missed her HBO concert special or 'Saturday Night Live' appearance, her GagaVille online game or fashion sale through Gilt Groupe, then perhaps you rode in one of the New York City subway cars decked out top to bottom with 'Born This Way' advertising…The extraordinary success of 'Born This Way'—it outsold the next 42 albums on Billboard's chart combined—are a testimony to Lady Gaga's appeal and the hard work of her business team, which devised one of the most extensive and savvy marketing campaigns ever mounted in music."

Her manager, Troy Carter, added that Gaga carried her end of the whirlwind schedule with equal vigor, arguing that "it wasn't marketing ploys that drove the success of that album. It was the quality of the content and Gaga's willingness to go around the world and play for the fans, do the promotion, do the TV shows, visit the radio stations and the club D.J.'s. There's a lot more of that than there are marketing ploys." Indeed, in spite of the assistance, the New York Times was quick to distinguish Gaga from her pop peers by admiring the fact that "unlike much of her competition in the pop charts, Lady Gaga is, by all accounts, a self-guided creation. While she collaborates with producers, designers and directors, her pop-culture juggernaut is not devised by committees or consultants."

Elaborating on her diehard work ethic, Vanity Fair reported that leading up to the album's release, the star "appeared on numerous television shows including Saturday Night Live, where she performed in skits and displayed a real comedic flair; she could easily host the show if she ever had the time. She had her own HBO special: the Monster Ball concert, live from Madison Square Garden. She appeared on the red carpet at last year's Grammys inside a 'vessel'—a semi-transparent egg designed by Hussein Chalayan. At the 2010 MTV Video Music Awards, she wore a dress made of actual meat (which was chemically treated and then enshrined in the Rock and Roll Hall of Fame). And this past year, she opened the MTV V.M.A.'s dressed as her alter ego, a guy named 'Jo Calderone,' who resembled either Ralph Macchio or Marlon Brando, depending on your age or point of view (more about that later, too). Wearing a man's Brooks Brothers suit (and prosthetic male genitalia inside her trousers), smoking a cigarette, and guzzling a bottle of beer, she shocked the audience and instantly made every female star in attendance who had pink hair or wore a contraption on her head look dated."

Quipping that unlike PrimaDonnaPop counterparts who might have complained about the rigorous demands of such a schedule, for Gaga, she used that fire for fuel creatively as she traveled the world, recording on the road night after night using inspirations she'd received in the moment of meeting and performing for fans to shape the album's conceptual direction, confessing to Vogue that "I can't imagine writing *not* on the road, in a way, because of the thrill of the show and their energy. I got so many ideas looking out into the crowd, like: 'I know what you want to hear. I know what you need.'" Heading off stage every night and onto the bus, Gaga explained to the New York Times that she kept her creative continuity constantly abuzz because "basically after the shows, I would go on the bus, and I would work all night. Then we would pull the buses over, and then I would get back on my bus and go to sleep on my bed, and then we would just keep driving. They would argue with me, and say, 'Gaga, we can't do your vocals right now,' with the sound of the bus and the reverberation...I get so inspired and ready to go, and I'm not the kind of person that can hold in my creativity; I always have to just do it right away." Gaga would add in a conversation with Vanity Fair that her devotion to her art would never entertain the distraction of back-stage competition of any sort because "I have always picked the music first. If anything gets in music's way, they're gone. My work has always been primary. It's not money and it's not record sales and it's not photographs. It's this invisible thing I imagine all the artists I ever loved could smell, that energy."

Acknowledging that this approach wouldn't have worked for an artist who wasn't a work-a-holic by her very creative nature, Gaga's manager Troy Carter argued that while Gaga's schedule might not have been "the ideal situation for most artists, for her it was great because she was able to tap into the emotions inside of those arenas. We would have a conversation backstage about something, and the next day she'd play me a song relating to the conversation that we just had! Watching the creative process with her is incredible." Describing Gaga's mobile music-making, the New York Times in 2011 described her 'Studio Bus' as "an extra tour bus holding a recording studio; her engineer, Dave Russell, and two producers, Mr. Blair and Fernando Garibay, traveled with her for a year." Sending tracks back and forth with one of her lead producers, Red One, he marveled at the focus she'd been able to maintain on the road during the album's recording because "our schedule has been crazy, so I've had to try and follow her everywhere. It's been a beautiful process."

Keeping her finger on the pulse of not only her fans but more broadly, the trends zigging and zagging around her on the charts, dance floors and live stages around the world as she traveled it night after night plotting her next musical move on wax, Gaga admitted in the course of discussing her broader vision for the album that "I like to be aware of the landscape," adding in the same conversation with Popdust.com that "I'm really keen on understanding how I can push the boundaries of pop music and still exist outside of it in some way. When I made *Born This Way*, I looked at underground dance music and the direction it was taking. Then, I thought about where I was in my life and what I was trying to express, and I tried to create this hybrid of underground dance music—which is the voice of my generation—and the spirit of anthemic, rebellious rock n' roll. That's what *Born This Way* is all about."

Delving into the musical mesh of stylistic sub-genres she was seeking to intersect within the album's broader sound, Gaga shared with FT Magazine in 2011 that "part of what the album was about…(is) marrying all of these genres and eclectic styles in a way that I am saying quite emphatically, 'I am a woman of theatre, I'm a librarian of theatre and I love all different kinds of music and all different kinds of expressions,' and the album is epic in that way that it takes you on this journey through all different kinds of expressionism in music…They function as both. I wanted to make sure that the album wasn't 'here's the balance, here's the up tempos.' I wanted it to feel much more like I experienced music when I was young; when you listen to a Pink Floyd song and even though it's slow, you're dancing."

Undeniably already a master at that art, as Gaga collected derivative rhythmic influences for the album's beatscapes, as she got down to work in the studio, she revealed to Ron Slomozicw of her process that, at all times, the singer-songwriter kept her musical mind open to anything that served her broader compositional concept of "bridging the gap in a few different ways, and it's mostly from a music conceptual standpoint, mixing the dance beats one second. Mixing retro dance beats with more urban melodies, and a certainly pop chorus. It's really about, in a very methodic way, almost choosing exactly what pieces of what I want to have in the record, and then watching it cross over, with my fingers crossed." Calling once again on the talents of producer RedOne, who had helped guide her last album to multi-platinum glory, and was excited their sophomore time around about bringing "cool beats and cool production" to the project, plugging himself right into the nerve center of her creative spirit as the producer who contributed "the majority…on both…Honestly, that kind of sound was created when I was with Gaga. So after that, the other producers had to adjust to that. You know?"

Clicking as potently as Amy Winehouse and lead producer Marc Ronson did, RedOne's collaboration didn't merely exist on an overdubbing level, but beneath the compositional surface as both put everything they could dig up creatively into serving "a song," as the producer revealed, ahead of any Protools bells and whistles, "it has to be a songwriter's song, almost like you feel you want to play it on a guitar and it will still sound good." Stripping down to the same naked honesty Gaga had from the first performance she ever gave, it was a requirement that for all her flash on stage she undoubtedly required of any collaborate in as private and intimate a creative space as the studio, and one where she affirmed on record, so to speak, to DJ Ron Slomowicz that she trusted Red One creatively with "the heart and soul of my universe. I met him and he completely, one hundred and fifty thousand percent wrapped his arms around my talent, and it was like we needed to work together. He has been a pioneer for the House of Gaga and his influence on me has been tremendous. I really couldn't have done it without him. He taught me in this own way—even though he's not a writer, he's a producer—he taught me how to be a better writer, because I started to think about melodies in a different way."

Returning to her roots—and reflecting just how inclusive her party was in welcoming any and all musical influences into its boiling musical melting pot—on top of all the dance, pop and hip hop players on the album derivatively, Gaga shared with Vogue that "there are some very rock-'n'-roll moments on the album, too: There's a Bruce Springsteen vibe, there's a Guns N' Roses moment. It's the anthemic nature of the melodies and the choruses." Rolling Stone would validate Gaga's authentic celebration of such influences credibly in her sound when they recognized rock & roll in "the way Gaga pillages the Bon Jovi, Pat Benatar and Eddie Money records of her childhood. In the 1980s, radio was full of tormented Catholic kids, from Madonna to Springsteen. Gaga clearly grew up on that stuff. She doesn't just give her Springsteen homage 'The Edge of Glory' a sax solo—she gets Clarence Clemons himself to play it."

When it was time for the superstar-to-be herself to step to the microphone to deliver the kind of knock-out vocal performances that a heavy weight contender in her position had to, the singer-songwriter delivered flawlessly with each vocal performance she stepped into the vocal booth to lay down. Speaking to her caliber of her talent as a recording artist, lead producer RedOne affirmed that "with Gaga, I almost have to fix nothing…She nails it, and we do it old school. If she does it wrong, she re-records it until we get it right. Instead of, 'It's alright, just do it and we'll fix it.' No. it's her singing it; I'm not fixing, tuning. I'm using her time in the best way because she's now big, and she's very busy. When she comes (to the studio,) I have her do a few verses and then I'll comp the best of the takes, and then she'll listen to it, and say, 'I can do this better,' and boom, it's good." Comparing and contrasting her vocal deliveries stylistically throughout 'Born This Way' with her previous studio LP, Gaga proudly shared with Vogue that her new material "is much more vocally up to par with what I've always been capable of. It's more electronic, but I have married a very theatrical vocal to it. It's like a giant musical-opus theater piece."

In crafting each of her vocal performances lyrically throughout the album, Gaga revealed to the LA Times of her process that each begins with "a feeling, there is a narrative, but the narrative isn't nearly as important the images are, sewn together." While needing no directional cues creatively from the competition in the style of pop songs she wrote, Gaga was smart enough of a pop operator to keep herself current on her peers' latest releases, reasoning to Popdust.com that it made sense as part of her process to "be aware of the landscape, but I'm really keen on understanding how I can push the boundaries of pop music and still exist outside of it in some way. When I made *Born This Way*, I looked at underground dance music and the direction it was taking. Then, I thought about where I was in my life and what I was trying to express, and I tried to create this hybrid of underground dance music—which is the voice of my generation—and the spirit of anthemic, rebellious rock n' roll. That's what *Born This Way* is all about."

Detailing the album's canvas of colorful vocal landscapes, Rolling Stone Magazine marveled in their opinion that "what makes *Born This Way* so disarmingly great is how warm and humane Gaga sounds. There isn't a subtle moment on the album, but even at its nuttiest, the music is full of wide-awake emotional details. The friendliest cut is 'Yoü & I,' her love song to a 'cool Nebraska guy.' She has been playing it live for a while, but who knew she would let Mutt Lange put 'We Will Rock You' drums all over it? Or bring in Queen's, Brian May to play guitar? All that excess just amps up the emotion in the song, especially when Gaga wails, 'There's only three men that I'm-a serve my whole life/It's my daddy and Nebraska and Jesus Christ.' Gaga loves overheated cosmic statements for the same reason she loves dance pop and metal guitars—because she hears them as echoes of her twisted rock & roll heart. That's the achievement of *Born This Way*: The more excessive Gaga gets, the more honest she sounds."

Another fan of Gaga's vocal talents was none other than legendary record producer Robert 'Mutt' Lange,' whose reputation for exhaustively meticulous perfectionism in the studio was not lost on the singer for a moment, and in fact, a bar of excellence she welcomed in her collaboration with Lange on 'You and I,' recalling to the New York Times of its recording that she in fact "told him that I wanted him to work me into the ground for my vocals." Lange asked for a guide vocal ahead of the pair heading physically into the studio, a nerve-racking exercise that wound up being so inspired Lange used it as the final vocal, and a performance the singer recorded after "I had about 30 cigarettes and a couple of glasses of Jameson and just put on a click track and sang my face off, thinking we'd redo the vocals."

Describing the LP's lyrical landscape topically, Rolling Stone Magazine continued in its gushing review of the album's universe of appeal in the topics it explored, "all over *Born This Way*, she takes on the big topics dear to her heart: sex, religion, muscle cars, her hair. She sings in French, German, Spanish and whatever language wants to claim 'punk-tious.' She seduces men, women, deities and dead presidents. ('Put your hands on me/John F. Kennedy'—hey, it rhymes.) And in 'Heavy Metal Lover,' Gaga purrs the immortal pickup line 'I want your whiskey mouth/All over my blond south.' Some songs are already familiar—at this point you could hum the Tarzan-boy yodels of 'Judas' in your sleep. But the singles gain resonance on the album, where they're surrounded by similar-minded psychosexual turmoil. 'Born This Way' pulls an expert bitch-stole-my-look on Madonna's 'Express Yourself.' But that isn't even the most brazen Madonna rip here: That honor goes to 'Judas.' And if you thought the Catholic angst of 'Judas' was over-the-top, check out 'Bloody Mary,' where Gaga does the Stations of the Cross to a Chic bass line."

Thematically, the album was as bold and provocative in its message lyrically as Gaga was in her own beliefs and teachings to fans, casting 'Born This Way' lyrically as a musical mirror of Gaga in her brave real life, sharing with the Guardian UK that "I'm writing more about pop culture as religion, my identity as my religion: 'I will fight and bleed to the death for my identity.' I am my own sanctuary and I can be reborn as many times as I choose throughout my life." Elaborating in even greater depth on the album's concepts she was exploring throughout the track listing, the singer revealed to FT Magazine that "I also sing about artifice and the surreal and magic. That's exactly what my new album is trying to combat and liberate at the same time, is the idea that I live halfway between reality and fantasy at all times because I choose to, and anyone can choose that, and I believe everybody has something so magical about themselves and why, as a society, are we so afraid of magic? Why is magic synonymous with artifice? Why is the fantastic synonymous with a lie? If art is a lie, then I will tell that lie every day until it's fucking true."

In creating her invitation to fans to come join her army of 'little monsters,' Gaga began by earning their trust through a complete confessional where bearing her own artistic soul was concerned, the singer underscored the importance of being in touch with vulnerability, explaining to Popdust.com that "I learned that to be a great artist, you must be emotionally very thin…Your tears and your anger and your happiness must be just under the surface of your first layer of skin…I like to say "emotionally thin" because it's much more dramatic. Vulnerable to me implies only tears…In my mind, to be a great artist you must be both private and public at all times. And yet I'm part of an industry that challenges the pop female head-on, guns a-blazing. I have to be emotionally thin but equally strong and impervious."

Pulling back the curtain on the writing of some of the album's specific songs, Gaga remained a mother who loved all her children, reasoning when asked to pick one favorite among her newest collection that, understandably, "it's so very difficult to say. I love all my songs so much." Beginning with the title track, the singer revealed that the song essentially wrote itself, recalling to Vogue that "I wrote it in ten fucking minutes, and it is a completely magical message song. And after I wrote it, the gates just opened, and the songs kept coming. It was like an immaculate conception." Another of Gaga's highlight songwriting moments on the album came with 'Russian Roulette,' which she proudly singled out as "such a powerful and perfect pop song," adding in the same conversation with Songwriter Universe that the song's title referred to "an urban myth where you take a gun and you spin the cage. You basically shoot it into your head—you are gambling. If I pull the trigger and play this game with a lover, I am playing this sort of morbid game. That is the gamble of dating, love, lust and sex. It's very animalistic and a very primitive relationship. Love can really fuck you up."

Taking on social and political territory with 'Americano,' Gaga shared of its muse with Vogue that "(that) is a big mariachi techno-house record, where I'm singing about immigration law and gay marriage and all sorts of things that have to do with disenfranchised communities in America. It sounds like a pop record, but when I sing it, I see Edith Piaf in a spotlight with an old microphone."

When her creative attentions were turned to 'Marry the Night,' a clever ode to her hometown of New York, the superstar told Howard Stern of the moment she first felt inspired to write the song that it came "that moment when I saw other people who were big stars and had mansions. I rented a place in L.A. for a bit in Bel-Air with a pool and a view of the mountains and I was like, okay here I go, this is what I'm supposed to do. But I was like, no thanks, it's been nice in the sun, but I'm going back to New York and marrying the night."

Rather than rushing to wrap work on the album, Gaga with F.A.M.E.'s success had earned the capital to spend as much time as she creatively required to finish the album, explaining to Larry King that "I wanted to give it some time, because even though it's finished, I really want to give my fans what they deserve, which is for me to promote and travel the world and give the new music to them in the most perfect and accessible way that I can. And I'm on tour right now, which means I would have just had to throw the album up against the wall. And it just cheapens the atmosphere, which I don't like to do. I like to do things that will—I want to go kiss every D.J. and radio director around the world again, like I did the first time. So that's the first thing. But the sound is—I couldn't possibly give anything away, because I don't want to reveal anything. But it's—the album was inspired by my new found understanding and love for my fans, a—a new found love and understanding for what they need, for what they dream about, for what they dream for our generation and for the future. And the album for me is an anthem for the new decade. It's an over-arching message."

As she was wrapping production on 'Born This Way,' Gaga seemed proud that her music matched her style so evenly as a soundtrack to more than just an image, but the full-fledged life-style she was selling her 'little monsters' all over the world, telling US Magazine that "I would say this album is just as over-accessorized as I am. You know there is something really epic and opus like about the record and it's meant to be this huge celebration of a sort of grandeur in terms of, you know—self love and self worship. This record as a stand alone, I wanted when you listened to it to not only be transported to reality but also to know that I've licked and touched and kissed and made love to every single note and melody and lyric on that album."

Released on May 23, 2011, Gaga embarked on a whirlwind press tour that took her from Oprah to The View, MTV to the top of the Billboard Hot 200 Album chart with a record-breaking MILLION-plus sales (1,108,000) copies sold in its first week at retail, outselling the rest of the Top 10 combined, and making her one of 2011's top selling recording artists.

The reverberation of the world going Gaga for pop's newest superstar was felt on charts all around the globe, with Japan reporting 180,000 copies of the album sold in its first week, 140,000 in Australia, 215,639 in the U.K., selling more than 2.5 million copies total in its first week of release worldwide. Ranked # 6 on Rolling Stone Magazine's '50 Best Albums of 2011' list and Grammy nominations for 'Album of the Year,' 'Best Pop Album' and 'Best Pop Solo Performance,' 'Born This Way' produced 5 Top 20 hit singles, including the title track (# 1 on the Billboard Hot 100 Singles Chart, her 3rd, moving 448,000 digital downloads in its first week of release), 'Marry the Night' (# 1 Hot Dance Club Songs'), 'Judas' (#10), 'Hair (# 12), 'You and I' (#16) and 'The Edge of Glory,' which peaked at # 3 on the Hot 100.

Lady Gaga: Born to be Free

"I am a songwriter. I am a performing artist."
—Lady Gaga to Barbara Walters, 2009

"Her act is a head on collision between performance, and art and underwear...Outrageous and outlandish and out of this world!"
—Barbara Walters re Lady Gaga's Live show

Chapter 7
Gaga Takes Over the World...

Once the record had hit stores and she was preparing to hit the road for what would become a live extravaganza with a Festival feel that eventually pushed Born This Way to upward of 8 million copies sold. With a lot on the line, Gaga's fortunes luckily paid off when her Born This Way Ball Tour became an instant sold-out hit after it launched at the end of April, 2012, covering the globe with 110 show dates. Still, for all the positive headlines she was getting in reviews, behind the scenes, Gaga was dancing and singing her heart out to buy her way out of what she revealed to the Financial Times was the shocking discovery "after the first extension of The Monster Ball, and it was funny because I didn't know! Why is everyone saying I have no money? This is ridiculous; I have five No. 1 singles...And they said, 'Well, you're $3 million in debt." Fortunately, Gaga Fever was proving to be a cash cow for the singer, who designed much of her branding personally and ran its commercial execution with an iron fist, wound up grossing a staggering $181 million over the course of its 2 year run.

Dazzling fans and critics alike with her live act that the Hollywood Reporter shared was so theatrical that "**Lady Gaga** straddled a faux horse, mounted a motorcycle, birthed herself through an inflatable, zipped vagina, hatched from an egg and dangled from a meat rack between massive slabs of beef. And somehow, the pop star also managed to change her costume 17 times…(in a) grab-bag, highly produced performance" that Time Out Magazine added lived up to the expectation for "freaky, sassy, salty-mouthed songstress to deliver radical performance art on an epic scale. The 'Born This Way Ball' kicks Gaga's visual thrills up to 11. The self-dubbed Mother Monster, whose Twitter profile describes her M.O. as 'when pop sucks the tits of art,' starts the show by clambering out of an enormous inflatable vagina before feeding herself into a meat grinder and shooting sparks from her bra in front of a 50-foot medieval castle. Hey, it's just another day at the office…(and) the 'Born This Way Ball' is a worldwide victory lap for a diva at the top of her game."

Having truly reached icon status overnight in pop culture, her position was qualified by Time Magazine's featuring her on their list of the Year's Most Interesting People, and that's precisely what happened to Lady Gaga in 2010 amid the global coming-out party she was making as the Millennium's newest pop superstar sensation. Admitting to Larry King that for as confident as she was in her brand, "I was so surprised (at the Time Magazine vote), I didn't even imagine that I would make the list at all. And I was so excited, and I am very blessed to have the wonderful fans that I do who voted for me." Feeling happily at home as a pop culture phenomenon who had arrived just in time as far as Gaga's fans were concerned, she told the New York Times in 2011 that the flight 'Born this Way' had taken from her head to the ears of her fans had been a surreal one because "the music takes on a completely different life once it enters the universe. The fans and myself begin to dictate the sentiment around the song, and how it's going to look and how it's going to feel and where it's going to be. It's wonderful. It's never finished. Pop culture is my religion, so to say pop culture is your religion you'd better believe your work is never finished, and that art is something that transcends, and it transforms."

A key to Gaga's success, in the educated opinion of MTV, had happened because her sound had succeeded in inspiring fans to "feel a certain way about themselves, so they'll be able to encompass, in their own lives, a sense of inner fame that they can project to the world, and the carefree nature of the album is a reflection of that aura." Crediting her fans as she would each and every time the opportunity presented itself as the fuel behind her fire, both creatively and commercially, Gaga drove home just how sincerely in a conversation with SHOWstudio.com where she declared that "as *an artist, I feel like I constantly have something to prove to myself or my fans. I have something to give or a point to prove: a message to prove. It's part of the process, proving myself over and over again. In that moment, I felt very free—very ready for a new proof, a new smell. A new age of my music.*"

Indeed a new age had arrived with the phenomenon of Lady Gaga, and one she seemed to draw the greatest validation from on the live stage, confessing to Larry King of the full-circle journey she felt she'd completed achieving this moment, *"I guess you could say it's always been my destiny to be a performer. I used to perform even just in restaurants with my family or in the living room. But it's been really a very exciting transition now that I get to do this for a living… It's a wonderful pressure. It's the most amazing pressure. It's not like any other kind of pressure. It's not under pressure, it's not water pressure. It's not pressure cooker. It's just wonderful. It's miraculous. I'm so blessed. I look out into the audience and I scream and cry, and we sing and we cheer and we dance. And I can't believe that 17,000 people are singing my lyrics or that even know my name…and I just refuse to stop. I probably should take a break and go on vacation. But I'd rather die on stage. Not under a palm tree."*

Giving fans a V.I.P. tour back months earlier behind the scenes of her live opus as she prepared to hit the road, in further breaking down her vision for a tour that would play before 2.5 million fans before it was all said and done, Gaga was clearly thinking that big from the start, explaining to Larry King that conceptually, "the show is a rejection of insecurity. The monster ball is in essence an exorcism for my fans and for myself where we sort of put everything out on the table and reject it. There is so much in the show about insecurity and struggle. And so many of my fans are really, really, really troubled. And I was really troubled. And I still am fairly troubled. So I guess you can say I relate to my fans in that way. And I choose not to hide from it. I'm not interested, Larry, in being a perfect placid pop singer that looks great in bikinis and is on the cover of every magazine. I'm more interested in helping my fans to love who they are and helping them to reject prejudice and reject those things that they're taught from society to not like themselves."

Preaching self-acceptance as a doctrine in both her live show's in-between song speeches to her audiences, the Hollywood Reporter described the superstar as in complete control of "her core audience of devout Little Monsters after two albums" on stage, adding that throughout the show, Gaga "doesn't so much perform as preach. Her sermons are built on the tenets of self-confidence and acceptance—both valuable qualities that Gaga's crowd seems apt to embrace."

The Guardian UK offered a sample from Gaga's rapport with her live audience, quoting a mini-sermon where she promised that "nothing we do together has a last or first time…you are eternity…you made me, little monsters. Tonight I want you to forget all your insecurities…what you feel makes you different in the greater destiny of life…I worked so hard to get where I am…just remember, I was so far beneath and now I'm so far above!"

Eager parishioners in her church, Gaga's fans were devout followers of her musical religion, one where the singer confirmed in the same article by The Guardian UK that her live show was indeed "a religious experience, but it's like a pop cultural church. I never intended for the Monster Ball to be a religious experience, it just became one…It's more self-worship, I think, not of me. I'm teaching people to worship themselves." Clearly addicted to the connection she'd made with her army of loyal fans, one she'd fought for her whole life through all the rejection through her school and starving artist years, the singer confessed candidly to Rolling Stone Magazine that "when I am not onstage I feel dead. Whether that is healthy or not to you, or healthy or not to anyone, or a doctor, is really of no concern to me. I don't feel alive unless I'm performing, and that's just the way I was born."

Wanting to give her fans a fully interactive experience that she first began designing as she was writing the songs for 'Born This Way,' Gaga revealed in the same conversation that "I always have a vision—when I'm writing a song I'm always thinking about the clothes, and the way I'm going to sing…How I move, that kind of stuff is written into the song. It's not just a song and I'm not just gonna stand on stage and sing," adding to MTV that "when I'm writing music, I'm thinking about the clothes I want to wear on stage. It's all about everything altogether—performance art, pop performance art, fashion. For me, it's everything coming together and being a real story that will bring back the super-fan. I want to bring that back. I want the imagery to be so strong that fans will want to eat and taste and lick every part of us."

A life-long lover of fashion who was finally being given the dream opportunity to design literally whatever she wanted with whomever she wanted, Gaga turned once again to longtime collaborator Nicola Formichetti, who she shared with SHOWstudio.com was *"really easy with Nicola and I, you know. He's one of my best friends and I love him so much. Nicola knows exactly who I am to my core—as a musician, an artist and as a girl: it's very easy. The whole Haus of*

Gaga works together, Matthew also. He's been creating clothes for me for years. We simply have a cigarette and a whisky and we look through racks of clothes—'This is nice, this is fabulous, put it on with this' and we go. It's very organic. There's no pretence or preconception, especially with photo shoots—we like to create on the spot. That's my favourite thing with Nicola, Matt and Nick Knight. We are all in the moment."

When asked to take fans behind the make-up and costumes to reveal her favorites, rather than picking one, the singer was gaga over them all, joking with her designer in the same conversation that *"there are so many, Nicola! How could you say that? My least favourite? I don't have one. You're amazing, Nicola—we always nail it. No regrets. Always moving forward. All the 'Bad Romance' clothing was incredible: the Schiaparelli inspired stuff we did, the McQueen stuff was amazing. We've done so much, it's hard to like or dislike anything. It's all part of who I am. It's like saying I don't like my arm—I don't like my arm any better than I like my foot, I like them equally, I need them both. It's an extension of myself. You can't say you don't like your arm or your foot because you need them both. I need fashion, I need music—I need them both."*

Inspiring her fans to come to the ball dressed in their own crazy costumes, Gaga added that from the stage perspective looking out on her audience mirroring the spirit of her own designs, *"they're all so great. I love when they get dressed up, it's so amazing. I get distracted during the show because I'm lollying, looking out into the audience. One of my favourites, which was quite committed, was this boy dressed fully as Kermit the frog because it was when I brought Kermit as my date. I guess he wanted me to think my boyfriend was in the audience because Kermit was my boyfriend at the time. I thought that was quite committed because he had the full head mask, everything and it was SO hot. It was back when I was doing The Fame Ball, so it was more a club—a nightclub—so it was so blistering hot. I was thinking "He's so committed in that suit." There's been some amazing ones. They're always amazing: the caution tape, the cone heads, the cigarette glasses burning in the audience while I'm jumping up and down and people* are screaming. The crystal dresses, the crystal hats, the mirrored outfits: I couldn't possibly choose one. They're all so wonderful. I liked his because he didn't make it, it was so difficult to wear and he was so hot, he really suffered for his moment. He suffered for his art, I really noticed him."

Excited to put her years of theatrical study to use in designing the backdrop sets of her stage show, Lady Gaga revealed to FT Magazine in 2011 that "I would say that if I could describe myself as an artist in terms of theatrical philosophy, I would say that I am Brechtian." Bringing her discipline for practice to the table as well in the course of rehearsing her live show ahead of gigs, Gaga expressed an all-business attitude where "I'm quite disciplined in piano rehearsal, voice rehearsal, dance rehearsal, putting the show together."

A requirement by the simple fact that "I am quite literally chest-open, exposed, open-heart surgery every night on that stage, bleeding for my fans and my music," Gaga added in the same interview with Vogue in 2012 that she found it "so funny when people say, 'It's amazing to see how hard you work.' We're supposed to work hard! I have the world at my fingertips. I am not going to saunter around the stage doing pelvic thrusts and lip-synching. That's not at all why I am in this. I don't feel spiritually connected to anyone in Hollywood makeup and a gown with diamond earrings on. I am just a different breed. I want to be your cool older sister who you feel really connected with, who you feel understands you and refuses to judge anything about you because she's been there."

Channeling "David Bowie and Prince" in the course of her live performance, Gaga described the music legends as "being the most paramount in terms of live performance" to Vogue, over the global journey that was the "Born This Way Ball", Gaga succeeded into fully growing into her own as a peer of the latter superstars, reasoning to The Guardian that with her latest tour, "I wanted to release my true identity, which I had not yet fully discovered. I used to stare at all the posters on my wall, many of which are the same ones that are on the walls of my dressing room now. I used to imagine what these legends must have been like and then I used to pray that whatever condition was impressed upon them I would also experience. In a lot of ways it was a prayer for creativity."

First embarking on an international leg of the tour that began on April 27th, 2012 in stadiums across the Pacific Rim, including Olympic Arena in Seoul, South Korea, AsiaWorld-Arena in Hong Kong, the Saitama Super-Arena in Japan, the TWTC Nangang Exhibition Hall in Taipei, Taiwan, the Mall of Asia Arena in the Philippines, the Rajamangala National Stadium in Thailand, Bankok, and the Singapore Indoor Stadium in Singapore before moving to the Vector Arena in New Zealand in June that also included a multi-city arena tour in Australia (Sydney, Melbourne, etc).

Beginning her European tour leg in mid-August and running through September, Gaga sold out Stadiums and Arenas over Europe's entire continent, including: Bulgaria, Romania, Austria, Lithuania, Latvia, Estonia, Finland, Sweden, Denmark, Germany, England, Ireland, the Netherlands, France, Switzerland, Belgium, Italy, and Spain, with longtime partner Lady Starlight opening these dates, as well as a tour leg that next swung into Latin America, beginning in Mexico City near the end of October before swinging into Puerto Rico and Costa Rica before moving on through November into Columbia, Brazil, Argentina, Chile, Peru, and Paraguay before ending December with stadium shows in South Africa and Russia.

Though clearly exhausted by the end of the tour's first leg and ahead even of the work she still had to do on the U.S. leg of the tour that would begin after the New Year in 2013, Gaga was proud of the international seas of fans she'd already won over, declaring boldly to The Guardian that her tour had already earned tens of millions of dollars because "I played show after show after show and murdered every single one of them!"

Next turning her attentions to conquering America with the same well-oiled determination and dedication that had dazzled the rest of the world, Gaga took her traveling carnival over January and February to multiple successes at sold-out arenas across the country, Vogue captured a snapshot of just why her show was among the top draws for the live entertainment dollar, beginning with a declaration that "if you have not seen Lady Gaga live, you do not know from Lady Gaga. In an arena, her music, which has often been dismissed as run-of-the-mill Euro-pop—somehow not edgy or deep enough—takes flight. It is as if each song were written for the express purpose of being belted—roared—in front of 20,000 people on an extravagant stage set with ten dancers taking up the rear. She manages to go from insane, over-the-top rock opera to syncopated dance routine to intimate, boozy piano ballad and then back again, through thirteen costume changes, without ever losing her total command of the stage. The fact that she has a huge voice, plays the piano and the stand-up bass, and wrote every lyric and melody herself adds to the sense that you are in the presence of a true artist who has only just begun to show what she's made of."

Lady Gaga: Born to be Free

"She just generates a lot of sizzle,"
—Joseph Germanotta, Lady Gaga's father,
New York Times

"My favorite is that Lady Gaga. She's the biggest. I'll tell you, I never met anyone with more talent than that lady."
—Tony Bennett to MTV

Chapter 8
Life as a Fashion Show...

When Sir Elton John crowns you "the most adventurous and talented star of our age," you know you're on to something, and her critics and peers universally agreed that Lady Gaga's "uncanny ability to mine decades of avant-garde and pop-culture history and twine them together in a way that feels like the future"—as Vogue mused—made her "a human synthesizer, a style aggregator, the perfect Wiki-Google-YouTube-era pop star." The first true global pop sensation since Madonna, Gaga's global appeal inspired the LA Times to rave that "more than any of her A-list peers, Lady Gaga makes a spectator sport of the entire pop-star experience, from her music to her pronouncements on social issues to her determination to wear the wackiest outfit possible every time she steps in front of the paparazzi. No one plays the mass media as cleverly as she has."

Having indeed become a full-fledged phenomenon unto herself by 2012, honing in on precisely why Gaga shone so much brighter than her contemporary pop sisters, the Times continued their analysis, reasoning that the "one of Gaga's gifts, maybe the one that most distinguishes her from the other talented women directing the pop zeitgeist right now, such as her recent collaborator Beyoncé, her fellow couture hound Rihanna or her rival in redefining blondness, Taylor Swift…(is that when) Gaga makes outrageous declarations…she backs them up, not only through her now famously provocative interviews but in her videos, her collaborations with designers and artists, her live performances and those infernally catchy hits."

A synthesized strategy where NPR recognized that "Gaga got where she is by working every angle, both inside her music and in the culture," as the world lined up to join her fan club, among those waiting in line were a whose-who of musical peers looking to collaborate, beginning with the aforementioned Elton John, who proudly announced to the Guardian that "I'd love to work with her in the future."

Still, unlike a fellow superstar like Lil Wayne, who earned the Guinness Book of World Records' #1 spot for collaborations after making more guest appearances on remixes and other artists' singles than anyone else between 2009 and 2013, roughly the same span of time that Gaga's superstardom had taken rise, the singer preferred to remain selective in spite of countless requests from peers across every sub-genre of pop, reasoning that her decision was sound because "I really want to stand on my own two feet," she told SHOWStudio. com in recent years, adding of her selectivity that "*I really don't want to do any collaborations, especially contemporary ones. I really want to stand on my own two feet: this album is my moment to create what will later be perceived in twenty years as iconic. That's what you should always be striving for. Today collaborations are not the same as they used to be: you collaborate to get your song on a different radio format or to up your record sales or to get people to pay attention to you by putting a star on your record—it's trivial and boring. I only collaborated with Beyoncé because I genuinely love her. There's no other reason to collaborate with someone. She's a real good person. She's my favourite in contemporary music. She is a lovely person, so kind, I just don't know how anyone could say one bad thing about her, to be honest. There's no reason to just put someone on a record because it's fashionable or good for you. You should do it because you want to."*

While she wasn't keen on singing on other artist's songs, she was happy to write songs for those artists to sing, a skill it turns out happened to be one that the superstar actually used as a foot in the door into the business, sharing with Billboard that "getting into writing for others happened naturally, because at the time, I didn't have a record deal…I don't have an ego about other people singing my songs."

Shedding some more light on her history as a songwriter for others, Billboard reported that "before she had hit records…(while) she was an apprentice songwriter working with a number of producers…trying to build a name for herself, Jody Gerson, who signed GaGa's publishing deal with Sony/ATV…(recalled) that she was driven to understand the publishing business from a young age. 'She interned at Famous Music Publishing before any of this, and even back then, she was famous for showing up for work in her undies…She blew me away from the moment I met her. She was already signed to Interscope, and we are so lucky to all be on the same page and have a great working relationship.'"

Spotlighting just how in-demand her brand of songwriting was by the time she had reached superstardom in her own right, the calls pouring in were a natural response to her streak of chart-topping hits, Gaga delved deeper into her process as a ghost-writer to Digital Spy Magazine, revealing that "I write all the time for other people but I don't like to say who I'm writing for. I just don't like to use other people to make me look cool. You know, I'm not a selfish artist and I love to create."

Among those pop peers that the singer seemed to have the most fun writing for, she singled out one of her own pop heroes, legendary trend-setter Cher, who Gaga penned 'The Greatest Things' for, sharing her memory of the dream-come-true opportunity with the Daily Star that "I wrote that song a long time ago, and I've never put it on one of my own albums for, really, no particular reason. I always write these concept records, and it just didn't fit in. But it's always been, like, this big, massive, beautiful hit record and everyone always says, 'Why don't you put that on your album?' And I said, 'I don't know, it just doesn't fit with everything else'. Cher heard the song and loved it and wanted to do it together. And I said, 'Fuck yeah, it's Cher!'"

Gaga got a different kind of kick out of writing for the Pussycat Dolls—a more targeted effort—that she shared with DJ Ron Slomowicz allowed her the opportunity to play the role of her muse mentally as she wrote, explaining of the process at the time she was working with the act that "Nicole Scherzinger has been in my head for probably the past three months. There's something that's very humbling about being able to write for a powerhouse group like that. Probably the biggest influence that they've had on me is making me want to be a better writer for them."

Elaborating on what elements make up the formula for a hit pop song in her educated estimation, the singer-songwriter began by reasoning in an interview with Billboard that "a hit record writes itself. If you have to wait, maybe the song isn't there. Once you tap into the soul, the song begins to write itself. And I usually write the choruses first, because without a good chorus, who really gives a fuck? I think most music is pop music. The mark of a great song is how many genres it can embody. It's about honesty and connection-look at a song like 'I Will Always Love You.' Whitney killed it as a pop song, but it works as a country song, a gospel song, everything. If I can play a song acoustic, or just on the piano, and it still works, I know it's good."

A nostalgic trip came in Gaga's co-writing sessions with Akon, who had first signed Gaga to his label, Kon Live Distribution, as part of a larger deal with her parent company Interscope. Co-writing 'Just Dance' together, which went on to win a Grammy Award for 'Best Dance Recording,' selling 9 million copies as a # 1 single. Clearly a fan of her co-writer and mentor, Lady Gaga glowingly gushed to DJ Ron Slomowicz of their collaboration that "Akon is a very talented songwriter to work with. His melodies, they're just insane. It's funny, I think about him a lot when I'm doing my melodies because he's so simple, and he's just been great. He keeps me on my feet, very grounded, but he also puts me on a silver platter, which is always very nice. So it's been an incredible influence. It's like every time you work with somebody that's better that you are, you become greater."

Equally smitten with his label's shining star, Akon proudly beamed to MTV that, as a collaborator, "she's incredible…She's brave. She's fresh. She's different. She's bold. She don't give a damn. You gotta take her as she is. That's the beauty of it. You're forced to like her the way she is without no extra stuff added."

Another of those select high-profile collaborations came on her ARTPOP album alongside R&B legend R. Kelly on the single 'Do What U Want,' a million-selling single that came about after Gaga recalled to MTV that she'd "been living in Chicago and spending a lot of time there, and that's where R. Kelly hails from. I was working on Artpop and I wrote 'Do What U Want' on tour. It was about my obsession with the way people view me. I have always been an R. Kelly fan and actually it is like an epic pastime in the Haus of Gaga that we just get fucked up and play R. Kelly. This is a real R&B song and I (said 'I) have to call the king of R&B and I need his blessing.' It was a mutual love."

Kelly, who co-wrote on the song once Gaga had presented it to him, telling the HipHopUpdate.com that "it was amazing, man. It's an honor to be working with *greatness*. When I say that I say it with all my heart, because she is great on the stage and off. She is so talented. I was doing a show and she ended up on the side of the stage with her friends watching. I didn't know what the hell was going on. I was wondering why people were screaming so loud! After the show she ended up giving me a call about a track and I was like, 'Hell yeah! Send it to me, let me hear what it is!' The next thing you know, it was all over the radio."

Whether they could book a studio appointment with her or not, the stars were still lining up like fans to gush about Gaga, and in the specific case of Madonna, to pay her heir apparent to the title of the Queen of Pop the high compliment of telling Rolling Stone Magazine that "I can see myself in Lady Gaga. In the early part of my career, for sure. When I saw her, she didn't have a lot of money for her production, she's got holes in her fishnets, and there's mistakes everywhere. It was kind of a mess, but I can see that she's got that It factor. It's nice to see that at a raw stage. I think Lady Gaga is great. When [she and daughter Lourdes] saw her, I actually felt a kind of recognition. I thought, 'She's got something. There's something quirky about her. She's fearless and funny, and when she spoke to the audience, she sounded intelligent and clever. She's unique."

Addressing the comparison in her own words, Gaga began with an obvious salute to the pop pioneer, telling Larry King that "I think Madonna is great. She's been a wonderful friend and very kind and supportive and amazing. And she's—she's such an incredible woman. And, you know, I get compared to so many people. And we're compared to each other, whether we're blond, brunette, black, white, straight, gay. But on another level, it's kind of funny, because my mother actually looks sort of like—like Madonna. And the older I've gotten, I look more and more like my mother. So sometimes I just want to say, it's not my fault that I look like her…She's wonderful. And there can never be another. So I have to think of even more ways to annoy and shock everyone, because she's done everything."

Seeking to pick the star's brain whenever she had the opportunity, the singer confirmed in a conversation with SHOWstudio.com that *"Madonna is a wonderful, wonderful person...She comes to my shows, I ask her questions, she gives me advice...She is so full of the most wonderful freedom and spirit and is so kind. Working with her has always been very exciting and fun: we have shared some wonderful, honest moments together."*

Honored for the opportunity to co-star in her very own "Saturday Night Live" sketch alongside Madonna—a reflection of true parallel that had come to link the two in the pop conscious—Lady Gaga recalled to Larry King of the event that "we had a blast! We were laughing. We're both quite militant about rehearsals. So we were driving everybody crazy, rehearsing over and over and over again. And SNL wanted us to go get ready for the show and we kept going. But she is so great. And of course the—no bad comparison to Madonna. She's wonderful. And there can never be another. So I have to think of even more ways to annoy and shock everyone, because she's done everything."

Gaga found the entire experience appearing on the show to be among her favorite perk moments of being a mainstream pop superstar, sharing with US Magazine following her appearance on the show in 2011 that "it was a nice surprise all the support I got for the skits and for being on the show. I was really super honored that **Justin [Timberlake]** and **Andy [Samberg]** wanted to be a part of so many of the skits, especially Liquorville and the Three Way. Cause those are super iconic for both of them as actors...I swear I wet myself I needed a diaper on set I was laughing so hard...it is nice to be able to show my fans the other artistic outlets that I am in love with and what else I can do and I went to theatre school for so long so it is a tremendous part of who I am and I can't wait to host *SNL* one day!"

She would do just that two years later in 2013, when, doubling as host and musical guest, Entertainment Weekly mused ahead of her debut that "It will, however, be interesting to see whether Gaga is as game as Cyrus was, and as willing to mock herself—because if anything will sink Gaga on *SNL*, it'll be an aura of self-importance. (Please, for everyone's sake: Leave the pretentious art talk at home for one night.) It'll also be interesting to see how Gaga's musical numbers compare to those we've already seen on *SNL* this season. In the past, she's elected mostly big, splashy, prop-filled performance pieces that helped her make a stage name for herself."

Gaga didn't disappoint on either front, passing the test skillfully enough for People Magazine to rave after the highly-rated show in November, 2013 that "it was everything that we'd hoped it would be," while Yahoo TV concluded that "like so many of her performances, (she) was fantastic. Sometimes it feels like Gaga's whole life is just one long performance—life as theater. So, it wasn't too much of a surprise that she could pull off some smart comedy. The energy she brought felt like a breath of fresh air for the show; in fact, this episode may just be the best so far of the season…It all started with the monologue (forget the cold open—it's dead to us these days). Lady Gaga, of course, sang and danced, a monologue staple that usually makes us groan. But she did a clever reworking of her hit song "Applause," which not only poked fun at her public image but also zinged how people get cheap applause by pandering to the audience."

Shaking her head in appreciative awe of the acceptance by and comparisons to these icons—ones she had looked up to her whole life for inspiration and motivation and now her equals in the context of fame—Gaga seemed to feel validation from the reality that "I could go on and on about all of the people I have been compared to—from Madonna to Grace Jones to Debbie Harry to Elton John to Marilyn Manson to Yoko Ono," reasoning in comments to Vogue that "at a certain point you have to realize that what they are saying is that I am cut from the cloth of performer, that I am like all of those people in spirit."

Life as a Fashion Show...

Arguably a club she had fought hard to gain membership into, vs. feeling like her socializing was for the cameras only, the singer seemed to feel that there was a genuine connection she'd made with stars like Cher and Elton John, revealing to ShowStudio.com that "its *been my experience in the industry that I have connected on a much deeper level with the most iconic and legendary people that I have admired. I have not connected with any of my contemporaries. I would say the one thing they all have in common, the legends that is, is that they are the nicest, most wonderful human beings you have ever met in your life. That has freed me. I used to be guarded in interviews, I'd sit there with glasses on and barely speak. I almost developed an accent at one point, I was so guarded and nervous. The media was trying to destroy me. I let it go much more when I got to meet the people I worshipped as a child. When you play piano with Elton John and you learn he's a fucking beautiful human being and the most wonderfully nice person, I thought 'I'm just going to be myself, I'm a wonderfully sweet person.' I don't always allow people to see that because I have to keep my hat on.*"

Continuing in the same conversation with what the contrast between acceptance by her peers and fans felt like, Gaga confessed that "when I'm with my fans, I can take my hat off, they know who I really am. I'm trying to say that loving, knowing, meeting Madonna has freed me. Meeting other people I love and to work with such iconic people: it can be terrifying. Hollywood is terrifying. I hate Hollywood—It's not real, it's completely fake and artificial. There's a tremendous sense of tension. There's no light heartedness about music or art anymore. I choose to exist in my own joy and just focus on the relationships I've got with the people I truly adore and respect. They are the most real and kind. It has influenced me most in the past six months, maybe a bit longer: everything happened very quickly for me. I've been working for so long on my music, art and performances and suddenly the whole world is watching you and trying to figure you out. You just want to put your giant stinking hat on to protect your music, your work and yourself. Meeting these people I'd give my right arm to have been around and learned from: I've discovered myself again. I've discovered my freedom, my security—myself. It makes me smile just talking about it."

Not only was Gaga a fixture on the celeb party circuit among the music industry's whose-who by this point, but perhaps even more poignantly—as a testament to the true scope of her cross-over popularity—the superstar had become a frequent flyer on the fashion runway, so to speak, courtesy of the immense respect she had earned with what The New York Times argued was a level of originality in her image—including an exclusive Gagafashionland. com website—that meant whether she was "clad in a dress of plastic spheres, a monstrous Dutch Boy wig with full S & M leathers; bodysuits and stilettos and a cage that caused her to resemble a walking armillary, Lady Gaga, a 23-year-old New Yorker, made better use of modern media than almost anybody. Lady Gaga mashes up. She subjects herself to a real-time version of Photoshop, studiously conjuring up an over-the-top creation built from bits of Bowery and Nomi and Jones and Bowie, but also Liberace, Joey Arias and Kylie Minogue."

Rolling Stone Magazine put an even finer point on why Gaga successfully conquered both worlds in the same time, recently noting that "since showing the world her poker face and hair bow in 2008, Lady Gaga's outfits have been talked about as much as her music. Attention-baiting or not, Lady Gaga's wardrobe changed the landscape of pop culture. The singer has brought high-fashion to mainstream consciousness, fostered a deeper respect for it as an artform…Throughout her career, Gaga has become a beacon of fantasy in pop and fashion. She's not only pushed the sartorial envelope with outlandish creations like that famous meat dress, she's also challenged ideals of beauty in both realms."

Explaining this sense of fantasy as part of her real-life identity, Gaga told Billboard that "I want to live the glam life, and my material is heavily rooted in that. There are all these places where art and self-expression and clothing can intersect, and on a cultural level, I

Life as a Fashion Show...

feel that music and fashion have always mirrored one another as a creative consciousness: a trend that is part of the zeitgeist. The way that people think about art, colour, fashion, music and visuals are connected in that way. They come from a similar vocabulary—they cannot be separate. I need fashion for my music and I need music for my fashion."

Treating her videos like their very own fashion shows, the Guardian noted that "today, a Gaga event is ridiculously lavish and expensive, what with the meat dresses, the dance troupe, the many designers, and the Haus of Gaga entourage. A recent photo shoot was estimated to have cost £150,000." Many among the top critics in the fashion industry have even convincingly argued that if Lady Gaga hadn't been destined for pop stardom, she would have instead become a famed fashion designer, with Elle Magazine UK arguing in favor of her credibility that while the superstar was indeed "a brilliant singer and a shrewd and commercial songwriter, but self-belief and a forensic understanding of fashion are what propelled her into orbit."

A superstar whose life absolutely imitated her art interchangeably enough for Billboard in 2013 to conclude that "Mother Monster is known for her outrageously creative and provocative outfits in day-to-day life, as well on stage," opening up about the true depth of her roots as a student of fashion in a conversation with V Magazine, Gaga revealed that "I myself can look at almost any hemline, silhouette, beadwork or heel architecture and tell you very precisely who designed it first, what French painter they stole it from, how many designers reinvented it after them and what cultural and musical movement parented the birth, death and resurrection of that particular trend. An expertise in the vocabulary of fashion, art and pop culture requires a tremendous amount of studying. My studio apartment on the LES, quite similar to many of my hotel suites now (knock on wood), was covered in inspiration. Everything from vintage books and magazines I found at the Strand on 12th Street to my dad's old Bowie posters to metal records from my best friend Lady Starlight to Aunt Merle's hand-me-down emerald-green designer pumps were sprawled all over the floor about two feet from my bathroom and four inches from my George Foreman Grill…Glam culture is ultimately rooted in obsession, and those of us who are truly devoted and loyal to the lifestyle of glamour are masters of its history. Or, to put it more elegantly, we are librarians."

Not merely hiring the top designers in the business, Gaga often preferred to design her own costumes, or work with designers she favored over the flavor of the moment, as happened when Rolling Stone Magazine reported that the singer had in fact "propelled the careers of formerly cult designers, like her long-time stylist, Nicola Formichetti—now artistic director of Diesel."

Taking a great measure of pride in playing a lead role on her design team, Gaga argued to Digital Spy Magazine that retaining that creative control is "incredibly important—you'd choke my entire vision if you took it from me. I design my clothes, I design my shows and I put it all together—it's a complete vision. I'm not interested in being thrown onstage in an outfit someone's picked out for me and just singing a song. I want to do something that people honestly remember. I want to walk onstage and have people say, 'I don't know what the fuck I just saw but I liked it.'"

Drawing creatively from her desire to—as with her music—"push the limits, push the boundaries as much as I can" when designing her outfits, Gaga was also aided by the fact that "I also really love—love the way I dress," confessing to Larry King that "it brings me a personal joy and satisfaction in my own life that I like to share with my fans. I also try to create things that are quite easy for my fans to replicate. Some of them not so much. But some of them are very easy for my fans to replicate, and that bonds us in a way. It's quite nice to have this connection to them outside of everything else." Expanding on why she loved allowing her fans to pick out her favorite wardrobe pieces, Gaga added in a conversation with Harper's Bazaar that "these are the pieces that have collected energy, joy, and screams from fans all over the world...The fashion I've acquired over the years is so sacred to me—from costumes to couture, high fashion to punk wear I've collected from my secret international hot spots. I keep everything in an enormous archive in Hollywood. The clothes are on mannequins, also on hangers and in boxes with a photo of each piece, and there's a Web site where I can go to look through everything. It's too big—I could never sort through it myself! But these garments tell the stories of my life. And then there are the tour pieces. This is the section that is *most* sacred to me...My fashion is my most prized possession for two reasons: 1) because it is a visualization of all the hard work I've put in to get where I am today; 2) because it is a legend to the encyclopedia of my life. It is exactly what I've aimed to seep into the artistic consciousness of people all over the world—that life is an art form."

Proving that she hasn't lost a bit of her Midas touch, in March, 2014, the Los Angeles Times reported in a feature story that "Elton John and David Furnish may have been the hosts, and the Elton John AIDS Foundation may have been the cause, but the talent that drew attention like moths to a flame was Lady Gaga, sweeping into Sunday's Elton John Oscars Viewing Party a few hours in and completely shifting the energy in the room. Even celebrity guests like Steven Tyler were left asking, 'What's going on over there?' when a massive crowd formed around the party's head table to catch even a glimpse of Gaga.

Security ultimately had to dispatch the crowd and then wrangle its ebbs and flows as numerous guests coincidentally found casual reasons to cruise toward the top table. The pop star, in sparkly strapless pink with a flowing chiffon scarf, the same number she hit the Oscars red carpet wearing, plunked down first between Donatella Versace and a radiant Jane Fonda (can we hope to look that smashing at 76?) before being joined by Elton upon his return to his seat. Heidi Klum, another head-table guest, sat just a few seats away as Gaga chattered along, especially with Fonda, before leaving at the end of the broadcast to hit Vanity Fair with the tiny-waisted Versace in completely different attire."

"I feel like 'ARTPOP' is what I've been making since 'The Fame'. It's what has defined me and my fans and we are claiming the music that is ours."
—Lady Gaga to NME, 2013

"Let's make 2013 a year where music/talent/artistry is more important than gossip/fanwars I respect all fanbases 4 their passion. Each song on ARTPOP was inspired by different types of adrenalin, so it's an expression of the various rushes, I want you to feel them."
—Lady Gaga, Twitter.com

Chapter 9
ART POP

The rollout for Lady Gaga's follow-up to the global success of 'Born This Way' wound up serving as a reminder that even a superstar isn't above being brought down to earth when the expectations surrounding a new album's release are set too high, a point that Harper's Bazaar drove home in a January, 2014 cover story that began by acknowledging that 2013 was "one of the most tumultuous years of her life…It's not always easy being Lady Gaga—and in 2013, it was especially difficult. For the first time since she emerged from the New York City City in 2008, Planet Gaga seemed in peril…(and) seemed to knock Gaga out of orbit."

Traveling back to the top of the previous year, the outlook for Gaga's highly-anticipated new album projected an opposite forecast, beginning with her own confident declaration in a live town-hall format chat with her fans on Sirius XM that "I refuse to do what I don't want to do, I am the artist and culture doesn't cue me. I cue culture."

Nobody could have cued Gaga for a greater reason to have such blind faith in how her fans would react to her third studio LP, especially consider it followed the record-setting success of Born This Way, which had been Gaga's own version of 'Like a Virgin' in the way it launched her into superstardom almost 25 years after the latter seminal LP had for Madonna, ironically her third as well. Eager by this point to steer away from such legacy comparisons as she was busy building her own, Gaga had everyone on her team sold of as much based on the track record of her visions coming true commercially.

Pointing to her record label head Jimmy Iovine's reaction at a listening party after "we had played him 40 songs," Gaga proudly recalled to Ryan Seacrest that the legendary record man was so hooked and wanting to hear more that "he wouldn't let me take my computer with me…At the end, we had a couple glasses of wine, and…Jimmy looked at me and said, 'Every record that you played me is better than the one that you played before it.'"

Eager as any artist would be in her position NOT to make 'Born This Way' the sequel, Gaga locked herself away in the studio, this time out with the bold conceptual goal of creating something that was "very risky," reasoning to NME that such a move only made sense based on her guiding philosophy that "if you're not taking a risk, you're not breaking any boundaries. It takes some time. New inspiration. New sounds…(and) new experiences," adding in a conversation on the subject with journalist Alex Galbraith at the time that "I'm really very fascinated with this transformation inside of me."

Taking fans farther down her creative rabbit hole into the center of her next musical metamorphosis, beginning with how the album's concept found its keyword, Gaga recalled to V Magazine that from the first moment the title popped into her head, "I instantly had an initial cosmetic experience with words, so I spent some time reflecting on exactly what it is that I wanted to say. When I'm thinking about the title for an album, I think about the marketing, I think about the cultural implication of the words, what the words mean. How the words will change the meaning after the music has been put out as well as the visuals. I spent some time and I kept seeing those two words, 'art' and 'pop,' put together in a reverse way, instead of Pop Art, which is the way I had always seen it. And then quite quickly, the more work that I did, ARTPOP became something that had a nice ring, you know? I had the right vibrational experience with the words and the way they sounded when I said them, with the way the work was coming out. Then I started to repeat them like a mantra…(so) when I was working, I was thinking, 'What does ARTPOP mean?' And then I started with the basic sense of it. Well, it could belong together. I thought about Pop Art and how the dominant subject matter was always the celebrity or the pop-culture icon on the canvas, and then I thought to myself, But what I have tried endlessly to become through my work is a celebration of my differences through art, with myself as the canvas, as opposed to me as the subject matter, being put on the canvas. I don't want to be an icon in just one form. I want to be an icon in many forms. So that's where it began."

With her concept now fleshed out and her tour officially over, as the spring of 2012 began, Gaga spied the studio as the perfect place to take a well-deserved break from the punishing schedule of late. One she desperately required both physically and mentally, Gaga offered a candid measure of just how far she was stretched with her recollection that "when I was finishing the (Born this Way tour at the end of 2011)…I was physically breaking. I was in a lot of pain, but didn't know where really. Anyone that's a performer and does these world tours, will tell you your body goes through a tremendous amount of stress, and I didn't know what was wrong…I have a strong threshold for pain, so I kept slapping myself saying, 'Get it together'…and I was going crazy cause my moves didn't feel the same and…the only thing that kept me going was the applause…and I was able to drown out the pain and finish the show."

Elaborating more indepthly to V Magazine about the extent the tour's tirelessly demanding physical rigor took in toll on her by its conclusion, the singer revealed that "I was in a wheelchair for three whole months. Before that I was basically on a cane and in a wheelchair on the tour in between the shows, trying to rest my body. It felt like my humanity was leaking on the stage, like gas out of a car or an oil leak. As my hip was breaking…and you know I didn't know it was my hip! Fuck if I know which part of my body it is that hurts the most. I don't know. I can't tell you that my hip hurts more than my back or my shoulders or my ass or my ankles in these fucking shoes or my tits. You know, after that 'Scheiße' routine, at the end, where I'm bouncing all over the place? I was on tour for basically five years once I was on the 'Born This Way' bus. It was the brunt of so many years of long-duration performances."

Manager Troy Carter confirmed that the severity of Gaga's injury was such that it had "a huge effect on our approach. We can't do as much as we would normally do," explaining to Anita Elberse that extra time was dictated by the star's extensive recovery from hip surgery, "having gone through the rehabilitation process…(we wanted) to keep her healthy and make sure she is not over worked, and can enjoy the process."

An important part of her healing process would come with taking well-deserved time away in a new refuge she had discovered away from the limelight in Chicago, her adopted hometown after striking up a romance with Chicago Fire star Taylor Kinney. So in love she even had motherhood on her mind, telling the Hollywood Reporter that "having my own kids will be like having three little monsters with me all the time—they probably won't be fans, in fact, they'll probably hate my music, who knows," one thing the superstar did know with 100% certainly was that she was head over heels in love. While not leaping up and down on couches with Tom Cruis-iastic enthusiasm when she appeared on Ellen Degeneres to discuss the relationship for the first time publicly, Gaga seemed to welcome the opportunity to pull back the curtain on some of what made the two such an instant fit, beginning with her revelation that the couple had competitively original personalities, such that "he's a hidden weirdo. He is extremely strange actually and we complement each other's weirdness. That's actually one of the first things he ever said to me. It's a Dr. Seuss quote that 'you find in someone else a compatible weirdness,' and it was one of the first things he's said to me."

In love it appeared with Kinney as much for their internal chemistry as she was by his disinterest in the constantly-hovering cloud of superstardom that now permanently followed Gaga everywhere, she was truly taken in—as she confessed to the NY Daily News—by the rare luck of meeting someone who "doesn't care about me being famous. I'm not famous to him, I'm his baby." Considering friendship one of the firmest foundations of their lasting love, Gaga gushed to Fashion Magazine that she indeed found it refreshing to be sharing her life with "someone that's not intimidated by the amazing people that are around you (or) by the love that you receive—that's love… At the end of the day, he's my best friend…and having your lover be your best friend, I mean, it's the best thing ever."

Choosing from the start to keep their romance as private a public affair as they could where the paparazzis obsession with her every move threatened to spoil their blossoming love, the couple avoided the spotlight, to the surprisingly effective extreme that the Huffington Post reported the couple's January, 2014 attendance of a Golden Globes after-party as "a rare public appearance." Kinney, responding for his part on The Today Show to the question of whether their collective celebrity got in the way of the opportunity to have the same kind of 'every day' romance any regular couple would, proudly described the day-to-day rhythm of he and the superstar's relationship as "normal, if you will, in that respect," adding that at the end of the day, "I'm a happy guy, I'm a lucky guy."

Dishing more dirt on a romance that took off right as Gaga's pop culture phenomenon did with the global whirlwind of promoting 'Born This Way,' the singer beamed with pride at her recollection to Fashion that "when we first met we were on the set of the 'You and I' video and I looked ridiculously crazy. It's this scene where he's electrocuting me to bring me back to life to the woman that he once loved. I've got these pins sticking out of my head and I'm wearing cork and I got no hair and I'm bald. Why he found me attractive just completely behooves me. We were in the middle of this scene and I remember that he kissed me and it wasn't scripted for him to kiss me and I was sort of like was um, you know, was that real or was that fake? And he didn't really say anything and that was fine by me and we kept filming."

Nearly two years later, it was clear the two had lasted in a business where so many celebrity relationships don't thanks to their success—as close as they remained—in leading independent lives and careers, an asset that Gaga clearly appreciated, confirming to the NY Daily News that "I'm lucky to be with someone who has a great job and he cares about his job…The way that it really works is, we trust each other. He's on his journey and I'm on mine, and we're gypsies—and then when we're together, we're really in love…We don't have any rules about calling each other at certain times. We'll go days at a time without talking. Then we'll talk every day. For me, the connection that I feel is so strong that it's so much stronger than physical. We're both very protective of our love as well. We treat each other with a lot of care and we're good to one another."

Setting up shop at state-of-the-art studios like CRC Studios in Chicago to stay close to boyfriend Taylor Kinney while he filmed his television show 'Chicago Fire' on location, Gaga described her "normal working day" during this "time off" throughout (what season, 2012 and what season, 2013) to V Magazine as a routine that begins when "I wake up—recently, a bit earlier—and I usually smoke and sit in bed and read. I put out all of my notebooks, computers, the music, pictures, art books, and I just sort of lie there and I smoke a bit. I look at everything and I really just look at it…I always think about the work a lot, but on this album I really spent a lot of time gazing, you know? Really gazing into the work and really thinking about what it means. How can I make it better? How can it become more original? How can I inspire them to see something that I don't even want them to see?…(So) in a typical day, I would do that for three to four hours in the morning…and then I start to make my calls…Then I will run or figure out a way to sweat, and then I'm usually at the studio."

Wearing and bearing her heart as nakedly as usual on her songwriting sleeve, as Gaga rolled hers up and started fleshing out specific compositional ideas that flowed from the 'ArtPop' concept down, she wrote from the same creative place at her core that had always driven her creativity, where at the root of it all, ahead of any commercial/single considerations, "the are was—and still is—the thing that drives me, you know? Pop is sort of my medium, the medium that I'm good at. But art was always the thing that drove me forward in these challenging and painful circumstances. I would always have the wings of high art kind of flying high above my back, lifting me up, and I could feel no pain, because I could feel the adrenaline of the future, of my artistic experience, and that was more important."

Staying prepared during this fluid period of songwriting to receive a creative brainstorm whenever one crashed her mind, night or day, Gaga confirmed that "I never know when I'm going to be sleeping or awake. I never know when I'm going to get an idea, and if I get an idea I have to work," adding in a conversation with V Magazine about what her waking writing hours are like as she's working on songs that "I drink Pellegrino, I'm a good Italian girl. I have Pellegrino with lime and a smoke. And I just lie there. Sometimes maybe green tea. I just sit there and look at everything. I get mad at the work, I get frustrated, I start getting really sweaty. I have a very emotional experience when I'm creating."

Touching on some of her proudest songwriting moments of triumph this sometimes challenging process produced, Gaga started with the album's title track, 'ARTPOP,' reciting to V Magazine some of the lines she felt best captured the song's conceptual center, she began with "A hybrid can withstand these things / my heart can beat with bricks and strings / my art pop could mean anything / we could belong together art pop.' It's all about the strength of coming together and having an exchange with someone through an artistic process. And in this sense this artistic process can ultimately lead to a pop-tistic process."

Turning to the writing of another of what would become the album's hit singles, the superstar songwriter shared with CNBC of 'Applause' that "its about this sort of place that we're in society where we're confused about famous people, we're confused about celebrities. We think that all celebrities are just taking photos of their ass on Instagram for attention and that this is what art is… It's not (about that), and it's also not what music is. It's not what showbiz is about at all, and I don't have to do all those things to curate my own legacy," adding in a Twitter post of the song's ultimate message that "I believe in show business. The 'Applause' is what breeds that thing that I love. When I know I've made you happy. When I know it was good." While she strategically placed the single as "the last song" on the album, the singer explained to MTV that she and her label chose to "put that out first so you have lots of time to learn the lyrics so when you're completely inebriated by the end of the album, the first time you listen to it, you, at least, know how to sing the last song."

Aiming from day one to write "music with no boundaries," once the individual phase of her songwriting was completed and came time to head into the studio, rather than taking the route many of her peers had by the same point in their career of hiring the top songwriters in the business to help craft 'hits', reasoning to the Hollywood Reporter that the move didn't make sense to her because "I find producers that have been in the industry for a long time to be very oppressive and very unsupportive of my natural talents because I'm blonde, female, and I have tits and an ass and I'm sexual onstage, so I must not know anything about music... There were experiences where they respect me as a musician, as an artist, as a songwriter, as a woman, and as a visionary. When I go in there, it's equal standing."

By rejecting convention in favor of recording only original compositions, Gaga was smartly retaining a certain measure of overarching creative control over the sound she was creating in the studio, emphasizing to NME that this was necessary vs. submitting to a producer's vision for the album because "nobody writes my songs for me! Every single song you've ever heard by me, I created from nothing with friends."

Her choice of friends reflected the singer's savvy for staying cutting edge, choosing to work with both legends like ever-current Rick Rubin along with some of the industry's hottest newcomers this time around, including Nick Monson and Paul Blair (DJ White Shadow), who jointly collaborated with Gaga in the studio on the majority of the album's tracks, including 'Venus,' 'Sexxx Dreams,' 'Jewels N Thugs,' 'Manicure,' 'Artpop,' 'Swine,' 'Do What U Want' and 'Applause.' Keeper tracks out of what co-producer Paul Blair estimated in an interview with Ryan Seacrest were "70 to 100 songs...we wrote...over the course of two and a half years," the team's litmus test for which songs were potential keepers came thereafter when Gaga added in the same conversation that they played the songs for a select group of trusted friends and waited "to see who gets drunk and takes their shirt off first."

Hammering this theme home more elaborately in an interview with radio station KIIS FM, the superstar emphasized the album's night-clubby vibe, Gaga explained that "it's my intention for you to have a really good time. I designed it for it to be fun from start to finish, like a night at the club in terms of the DJing aspect of it." One of those DJ collaborators, DJ White Shadow aka Paul Blair, felt Gaga was the perfect pop star to infuse the DJing influence credibly courtesy of her continually current popularity on his DJing scene, confirming to fansite Propagaga.com that "she was such an overpowering force when I was a DJ and playing her remixes. She was just everywhere. I'm not a huge pop music guy. I respect her, she's the hardest working person I've met in my entire life—a fucking genius. For lack of a better word, she's just a G. She works non-stop. You have to respect that. I don't think people give her enough credit for how hard she works and how she tries to do stuff that is different than everybody else. It would be really easy to make another 'Just Dance' and I'm sure people would love it and we'd sell a ton of records. Neither one of us wanna do that. We want to make stuff that people like, but it's for you guys first. We never sat down and were like 'Let's make this song so we can sell.' I think we both see eye to eye on that and she works hard to make sure it's good music."

Wisely keeping a nightclub vibe going throughout an album that continued to credibly celebrate her roots as a DJ, Spin Magazine was impressed convincingly enough to devote an entire feature to an in-depth deconstruction of the production of the aforementioned single 'Venus.' Beginning by paying the singer the high compliment of noting that she had "already proved her underground bona fides via an appearance—two of them, actually—at Berlin's Berghain club," the legendary alternative rock magazine added as they dug deeper that "that's nothing compared to the subcultural excavation she undertakes with her new single, 'Venus,' co-written by Gaga and core *Artpop* collaborators Paul Blair (DJ White Shadow), Nick Monson, Dino Zisis, and Hugo Leclercq—a.k.a. the 19-year-old French EDM producer Madeon—contains an officially licensed sample of 'Rocket Number 9,' recorded by the French synth-rockers Zombie Zombie. For fans of France's dance-music underground, that's pretty unexpected. Zombie Zombie, the duo of Etienne Jaumet and Cosmic Neman, are known for a darkly seductive sound that draws from Krautrock, French cosmic rockers like Heldon, and the horror soundtracks of John Carpenter. (In 2010, they even released a mini-album of John Carpenter covers.)

Nationality aside, in terms of sound and visibility, the duo—signed to the Parisian independent label Versatile, home to left-field house artists like I:Cube and Chateau Flight—is worlds away from the buzzing-in-every-way Madeon, a rave-pop prodigy whose peppy, sidechain-heavy sound is halfway between Deadmau5 and Daft Punk...But as far as curveballs go, the mere presence of Zombie Zombie pales in comparison to the fact that 'Rocket Number 9' is actually a song by the legendary jazz musician and avowed intergalactic traveler Sun Ra. Originally released on 1972's *Space Is the Place*, the song brackets incendiary, lickety-split ensemble melodies, mind-bending soloing, and a long, abstracted breakdown with a chanted chorus—'Rocket Number 9 take off for the planet Venus / Zoom! Zoom! Zoom! Up in the air!'—more in keeping with Raymon Scott's Saturday-morning cartoon soundtracks.

In addition to the Zombie Zombie sample, Gaga borrows Sun Ra's chorus wholesale and folds it into new lyrics addressed to 'Goddess of Love, Venus,' coming up with a song that's very *Barbarella 2.0*. The distance between Venus and Saturn, where Sun Ra said he was born, may be vast, but leave it to *Artpop* to blaze a shortcut."

Delving more directly into the song's basic writing, GAGA shared with a journalist while on the set of the single's official video shoot that "a lot of things inspired Venus, actually. I wrote this song when I was first thinking up ARTPOP. I actually thought of it when I went back home to be with family after surgery. I had to lay in bed for days and days. I have a bookshelf next to my bed, in arms reach, and I grabbed one of the books I loved as a child. It was some book about the ocean. It had lots of photos and graphics of all types of sea creatures. I hadn't looked in this book since I was very little, so I pulled up Youtube and started looking up the animals in the book. There are animals in the ocean that can change colors, flash and do all sorta of things to stay alive and a light went off in my head."

As critical acclaim from precisely the stylistic circles she was aiming to win over continued to build online, many of the most popular electronic dance music bloggers and websites were eager to celebrate the fact that many of the sub-genres biggest underground stars were not gaining mainstream recognition and respect, DanceAstronaut. com also threw some Gaga's way with their acknowledgement that "over the course of her creative growth between 2011's *Born This Way* and the spawn of *Artpop,* Gaga developed an admiration for new producers to the scene—avante garde talent that could help push her futuristic vision for popular music with her next album. Among those producers are Anton Zaslavski and Hugo Pierre Leclrcq. But let's just call them Zedd and Madeon. And combined they're responsible for more than one third of the record's tracks."

Honing in particularly on French DJ Madeon's impressive influence on shaping the album given that he had reached such a level while still only in his teens, the website added in their coverage of the album that "his *Artpop* contributions appear more advanced than even his strongest efforts—and they're nothing like the crisp, colorful music that currently fills his repertoire. 'Venus' reveals an edgier persona of Madeon with a hard hitting core, an unexpected bite, and grandiose emotion where appropriate. 'Mary Jane Holland' is a genre-defiant production lead by electro-rock grunge—with the exception of the French house influence, all elements are foreign to any previous standards he's set for himself.

Contributing to the album's finale, Madeon helps Gaga take the mood of *Artpop* from ballad to anthem all with one turn-around song. Producing with both sentimental and inspiriting elements, 'Gypsy' sounds like Madeon at his best without sounding like Madeon at all. His wide ranging execution on *Artpop* is an impressive feat for any musician. But it's not that he's drifted from his comfort zone—it's that a comfort zone may not even exist for Madeon—magnifying the already great potential and expectations that he's garnered in his teen years."

Speaking for his own part on the excitement of working with Gaga in crafting the aforementioned tracks, Madeon felt the fit was perfect, explaining to MTV.com that it was a good match-up because "I've always been in dance music, but I've always been a pop fan at heart," he told MTV News. "I've always wanted to work with pop artists and my #1 on my list was Lady Gaga. So when I had the opportunity to do that, I was really thrilled. And, yeah, it's really fun to be introduced to worlds of radio and charts and all those new [concepts] that you don't quite have when you're just DJing and doing dance music. So it's been a crazy experience for sure."

Turning to the creation of another of the album's singles, 'Aura,' to highlight another collaborator from the DJ community's contributions to the album's creation, German DZJ Zedd described the nature of his vibe in the studio with the singer as "experimental," expanding on their process in the same conversation with Rolling Stone Magazine that once in the studio, collaborating with Gaga is "amazing because she does not have to please anyone, and she is who she is. Her first idea of how we should approach the music was just to be completely open—nothing is too crazy. Whatever is dope is dope. We do whatever we want, and we don't have to make a song that's 3 minutes and 30 seconds just to fit the radio."

Embracing the creative freedom the superstar's status had earned her by this point in her career, Zedd added to Digital Spy that "I think GaGa did exactly what she wanted with *Born This Way* and I think that's the only way you can be a true artist. It's the same with *ARTPOP*, she's just doing what she wants to do. She wants me to do the craziest songs I can possibly do. I'm not thinking about fitting a shoe on the right foot. We're doing something completely unique and what we think is new. She's not been saying, 'You need to please my fans so make the songs sound like this', we've just made music."

Working together all over the globe, a necessity born out of the demands of Gaga's touring schedule, the producer felt the experience was uniquely organic in a day and age where many artists are sent already-produced instrumental tracks to record vocals over, Gaga and Zedd built their songs from the ground up, recalling in the same conversation with Digital Spy that "we tried to avoid working solely over email as it's hard to bounce off each other's ideas that way...We've actually been together for most of the sessions. We spent a few months together in LA a while ago and then I went on tour with her in Asia for almost two months. After the shows we would set up a studio and work on the track."

A musical melting pot boiling over with cutting edge blends of styles "coherently blending R&B, techno, disco, and rock music," in the esteemed opinion of Billboard, by the time it was done, DJ White Shadow felt the album as a whole was "another step on the ladder, it's another step forward. It's different, it's a different record," adding in the same interview with MTV News that "we didn't sit down and say 'ARTPOP has to be this'. It's like that's how she's feeling at the time. I think it's a really fun album. There's really fun stuff on there. We didn't make 15 trees; we made a forest. She's writing every single song, so they're coming from her."

Even as Gaga was working around the clock in the studio up to the last minute putting the final touches on the production of 'ArtPop,' her handlers on the label and management side had been working for months devising about as sophisticated a marketing strategy to devise as any Michael Jackson album launch in its heyday. Confirmed by longtime manager Troy Carter in an elaborate interview with Harvard University Business School Professor Anita Elberse that—in line with Gaga's superstar status—"we were treating it like a summer blockbuster movie, reinventing the way that albums are typically launched," her manager added that the team's strategy from day one involved a "launch (that)…was all about going as big as we could go globally, and getting the word out through a lot of non-traditional partners."

Reasoning that their super-push to think outside-the-box was dictated by the reality that "today's consumers are just inundated with information," Carter argued that even amid the backdrop of Gaga's global stardom, "something new launches every day. We live in this 24-hour, 7-days-a-week news cycle, and there's so much information being given to us at any given time. The question is how do you grab a portion of that mind share? We need people to know that we have an album coming out on a certain date, which involves giving them multiple impressions—whether they are getting coffee in the morning, or getting in their car to go work, or watching television. The goal is to capture mind share in a noisy environment."

Even with some of the savviest minds in the business working as part of her marketing braintrust, it was clear the buck ultimately stopped with Gaga, who Carter confirmed in the same conversation "plays a big role. She writes all of her own lyrics and music, so it always revolves around personal stories and experiences." Studying current trends as well as those that drove past Gaga LP launches, her management felt it was important to make a bang that packed reverberations in the context of Billboard's constant competition week in and out with pop peers' labels pouring rival promotional dollars into their artist's releases in the hopes of snatching record sales from his client, Carter underscored that "one of the things we learned from the last album cycle was to make this about more than just the first week of sales. In the media industry, everyone is looking to front load, pushing for a high opening gross for a movie and high album sales in week one. But what about the second week, and the third week?

We are looking at how can we stretch this campaign. Instead of just layering it with partners at the top of the campaign, pushing for high first-week sales, we want to make sales last longer…Each album cycle changes because the market changes. We're looking at the other albums being released, the public's sentiments around the artist…all of those factors shape our messaging and our marketing…We look at key milestones during the album cycle. We know that opening up the album is one milestone, but Christmas is a second milestone, and the announcement of the tour is another, just as the actual start of the tour is one. We are looking at how we can take partners from one point to the next, throughout the next year and a half."

Highlighting social media as an indispensable resource, social media provided in getting the wheels turning on the aforementioned roll-out effort that Gaga's team spent the summer putting into place, the superstar viewed the digital medium as the portal through which all of her fans could simultaneously experience the full dimensions of the multi-media experience that was 'ArtPop.'

Seeking to set a specific date when Gaga revealed to V Magazine was "the day that all of the fans in all countries around the world would be able to get access to the music at the same time," she added of the challenges inherent in coordinating such a feat that "it had a lot to do with delivering copies and making sure we had enough time to upload the music to all the servers worldwide. I was trying to think of everything. When would be the best time in my fans' lives? And if I tell them two to three months before the album comes out, it gives them a few months to save their money as well. You know, I care about that too. I want them to have time to save their money so that they can buy it. I don't expect them to be rich. I don't expect them to just have the money to buy the music. In this age, buying music is sort of an old thing, and the app is the new generation of a physical experience with music through digital interaction."

While the singer acknowledged the importance her online following played in driving record sales, for the singer on a more organic level,

Gaga seemed thrilled with the ability via the technology for her fans to share the same experience in the same moment, emphasizing to V Magazine that amid all the hype and hoopla, "the most important thing for me is that every fan has the ability to access the work at the same time. If they can't experience it together, it deflates the meaning of the work, which is that art and pop belong together.

So the moment for me is only explosive if art and pop are together in one instant and the fans get to experience it together in one instant for the first time. It's like an ultimate explosion of experience for them—where they get to touch and feel the music and art—with a philosophy and framework behind it that really allows them to understand the kind of shape-shifter performer that I am. I'm someone that wants them to view me not only as a figure with many wigs, but as a figure with many wigs who has a skin tone of many colors, with nails of many paints, and the shoes of many people, with the heart of many thieves and many wise men, and an ability to transform emotionally as well as intellectually as well as humanly. I create the work so that they can have a physical and virtual representation at once. That is what ARTPOP is all about, to bring the technical aspects of being a performer together with the metaphysical, and to ask the fans to look and experience both of them at the same time."

Celebrating the brilliance of empowering her fans by giving them an interactive, hands-on role in the album's launch, Forbes reported ahead of the launch that "since Lady Gaga came on the music scene in 2008, she has always been 'fan-centric.' Now with her third album, *ARTPOP*, about to release on November 11, she is rewarding her diehard fans with ways to be directly involved in the excitement of getting the word out on the new release. So how exactly does one approach their first set of new music in two years and after a lengthy absence from the limelight? If you're Lady Gaga, then you leverage the strategic asset you have been building for years: your passionate fan base, the Little Monsters. They number in the tens of millions, with over 40 million fans on Twitter and 60 million on Facebook."

Taking advantage of the booming 'smart' technological possibilities available via iPhones, tablets, etc to make her fans feel part of her creative process via an exclusive fan-focused app Gaga and her team had "been working on for two years" she revealed to the Hollywood Reporter, the legendary industry paper described 'PETGA' as a "free app with a pet-Gaga who guides fans into remixing and scratching her new tracks, creating animated GIFs and connecting to her Little Monsters social network, with options to live-deejay music with other fans in the future. Each user's 'aura,' or abstract avatar scanned via the device's front camera, changes colors based on activity on the app."

Elaborating on the actual nuts and bolts that went into developing the first-of-its-kind app, manager Troy Carter explained to Harvard University Business School Professor Anita Elberse that they'd successfully "built an app for Apple and Android phones that will give a richer experience around the music. We set out about a year ago to start building it with some incredible engineers and story-tellers. It will be a free app. Version one will be released with the album, and two or three more versions will come out over the next few months. We think such apps are the future of our business. It is an expensive proposition—we want to give her fans an experience they have not witnessed before."

Carter added in the same conversation that other roll-out co-ops the team was excited about included "the partnership with Zynga was great in that it led to hundreds of millions of impressions through *FarmVille*. The $0.99 Amazon promotion was very effective, too. The media value by itself went a long way. Media around the world covered the story about the affordable price and painted us as Robin Hoods. To be able to break the album like that was a fun experience for us and for our partners."

By the time they were ready for the roll-out to begin, the team had succeeded in raising such a buzz that the Huffington Post matter-of-factly quipped by the end of the summer that "there's just one way to escape the blitz surrounding Lady Gaga's new album: completely unplug from society. To kick off the release of her new album, "Artpop," this week, the entertainer, never known for understatement, has been omnipresent. She began with a huge release party Sunday where she debuted Volantis, billed as the "world's first flying dress." She floated about 6 feet above the floor before performing at the event, streamed live on Vevo. The next day, she opened pop-up "Artpop" stores in New York and Los Angeles, where Gaga-related merchandise was sold, and she was one of the main honorees at Glamour's Women of the Year ceremony. On Wednesday, she was due to appear at the opening of an H&M store in New York's Times Square. She's scheduled to tackle hosting and performance duties on NBC's "Saturday Night Live," and she redesigned the Life section logo of USA Today in her image—the first time the newspaper has had a celebrity do so. The newspaper also featured an interview with the superstar. And a concert special with Ryan Seacrest is set to air on the CW Network next week."

After so much time off, as she began prepping for the world-tour that would follow in support of her newest studio LP, Gaga—after taking a much-needed break from the road—confessed to Ryan Seacrest that "I had to get back in shape, but to be fair I have never cared about my weight...it's other people that care. I do fear at times that if I'm not in shape, people will talk about that and not my music," adding to the Hollywood Reporter that by the time she was done, "I lost about thirty pounds to this album—I'm sure you saw the pictures."

Her chief motivators and biggest cheerleaders, as always, were her fans, revealing in a conversation with V Magazine that *"I see my fans and how they become so excited by music. They are obsessed with what I'm creating and then in some way they find an inspiration in their own life, where they're creating something that they become obsessed with. And they're no longer obsessed with the icon, they're obsessed with themselves. When I'm on the stage, everything begins to fade and*

I relax. I feel the applause. I feel the energy of the room. When I walk onto the stage, the first thing I think is, 'Find the energy.'"

Critics certainly seemed abuzz with positive praises for the album ahead of its release, with Billboard ranking the album as among the Top 15 of 2013 and hailing it as "often euphoric" and offering "fans her most sonically and lyrically diverse album to date." Spin Magazine celebrated the "seriously banging pop" of her latest musical morphing, while the LA Times warns listeners not to "underestimate Lady Gaga" as she began promoting a record where Time Out argued the greatest "triumph of 'Artpop' is that it mixes its palette of influences in such entertaining ways."

Reflecting just how mainstream a listening audience she had lining up to review the LP ahead of its highly-publicized/promoted release date, USA Today raved that ARTPOP "bursts with Disco energy," highlighting their admiration for the pop star's "fearlessness" in producing a sound that was "undeniably relentless" throughout its 15 tracks.

For as amped up as she was heading into the album's November 6 release date, sadly, Gaga and her team's hard work would be only marginally rewarded in terms of meeting or exceeding the explosive first-week sales of a million+ that her last LP had produced, selling an underwhelming 258,000 copies. Equivalent to a much-hyped summer blockbuster movie that opens so far beneath studio projections that it's immediately shoved into the write-off category, it was clear by the album's second week in stores—where it witnessed a staggering 82% drop-off from first-week sales, with Business Week reporting that "despite all the fanfare, *ARTPOP* isn't selling. The album sold just over 250,000 copies in its first week, putting it behind Katy Perry's *Prism* (286,000 copies) and Miley Cyrus' *Bangerz* (270,000 copies)—far below the expected 350,000 sales touted before its release.

Interscope may lose so much money on the album that unconfirmed rumors of layoffs are circulating…For someone who once seemed able to churn out hit songs in her sleep—*Bad Romance* has sold over 10 million singles since it came out in 2009—*ARTPOP* feels more like a fizzle." Forbes Magazine profiled a cover story on "the deflation of a superstar" while Entertainment Weekly added that while "as pop, the album is a well-executed and entertaining tour of Gaga's tried-and-true tricks. But as art, it falls short when it comes to one basic function: making an impression."

Racing to stand behind her product and put as positive a public spin as possible on what must have been a panic going on behind the scenes, Gaga insisted the best was yet to come, assuring her fans in a blog posted to LittleMonsters.com that "the next few months of 'ARTPOP' will truly be its beginning. Because those who did not care about 'ARTPOP's' success are now gone, and the dreams I have been planning can now come to fruition."

Shaking off the numbers in favor of focusing on the art, the singer likened the making of ARTPOP to "a long love affair. And it's not over, it's so wonderful. I have this endless experience with the music, where I'm so proud of it throughout its growth and duration. Even though I have moments with it where I'm disappointed, they glaze over."

As heads must roll amid such a public disaster, Gaga's manager Troy Carter became the logical sacrifice, with Gaga blaming Carter post-ArtPop's flop as being among "those who have betrayed me gravely mismanaged my time and health and left me on my own to damage control any problems that ensued…Millions of dollars are not enough for some people. They want billions. Then they need trillions," adding to Harper's Bazaar that "I felt very taken advantage of by people I trusted…Sometimes I get this gut feeling about people—maybe I sense a hidden agenda or that they care for the money more than the message. I wish that I'd listen to that feeling instead of waiting for the truth to rear its ugly head. I'm a smart girl. I'm loyal. But sometimes I'm too loyal. I'm not loyal enough to myself."

Carter responded on a more personal note that the shock of waking up after "you work with somebody every day, and then all of a sudden they're not there anymore," adding in the same comments to FastCompnay.com that "I don't think you're ever prepared to sever that deep of a relationship."

For as welcoming of the public spotlight as she'd been in the first phase of her career, by the end of 2013, it was clear the scrutiny following her album's commercial disaster had taken a real toll, with the singer revealing to journalist Alex Galbraith for possibly the first time that "the truth is that it is very hard to be famous. It's wonderful to be famous because I have amazing fans. But it is very, very hard to go out into the world when you are not feeling happy and act like you are because I am a human being too and I break."

Cycling deeper into a depression as the year grinded toward a close, as Gaga began processing her first real stumble as a superstar, in early 2014, she confirmed in her conversation with Harper's Bazaar that "I went through a rough time last year…(and) became very depressed at the end of 2013. I was exhausted fighting people off. I couldn't even feel my own heartbeat. I was angry, cynical, and had this deep sadness like an anchor dragging everywhere I go. I just didn't feel like fighting anymore. I didn't feel like standing up for myself one more time—to one more person who lied to me. But January 1, I woke up, started crying again, and I looked in the mirror and said, "I know you don't want to fight. I know you think you can't, but you've done this before. I know it hurts, but you won't survive this depression."

I really felt like I was dying—my light completely out. I said to myself, 'Whatever is left in there, even just one light molecule, you will find it and make it multiply. You have to for you. You have to for your music. You have to for your fans and your family.' Depression doesn't take away your talents—it just makes them harder to find. But I always find it. I learned that my sadness never destroyed what was great about me. You just have to go back to that greatness, find that one little light that's left. I'm lucky I found one little glimmer stored away."

That glimmer would come in the form of a source of light provided by her family, boyfriend—who she confirmed to the NY Daily News had "stuck it out with me for a very long time, through drug habits and all those sorts of things, so he's a really lovely, amazing person"—and her most die-hard fans. Giving them a first-hand look inside just how hard a time she was going through as the shadow of ArtPop's fallout continued to reverberate throughout the industry, Gaga revealed in her conversation with Harper's Bazaar in January, 2014 that as her depression deepened over the break-up with manager Troy Carter, "I asked my mother: 'I work so hard. I never stop. I never say no. Why doesn't this person love me, Mom? Why was this person willing to hurt me to help themselves? Why wasn't I enough? Why is money more important than me?'

She reminded me to forgive others for not seeing God where I see it. I see God in my fans. She said, 'You're hurt because you don't operate this way. You are fiercely protective of your inventions because you are your fans.' She helped me understand my own feelings. When someone has pulled the wool over my eyes, I feel that they have pulled the wool over the eyes of millions of fans around the world. She helped me to forgive. You can't force people to have the same world consciousness and awareness as you do." Ultimately, Gaga found her greatest refuge out on the road where she told the Hollywood Reporter ahead of kicking off the ARTPOP world tour in the spring of 2014 that "I love performing live so much, so that really saves me."

Lady Gaga—International Superstar

Lady Gaga on the Red Carpet at the 2014 Grammys

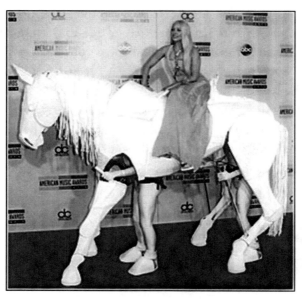

Lady Gaga, known for her grand entrances, didn't disappoint at the 2013 American Music Awards, riding in on a human-powered horse

Lady Gaga—International Superstar

Lady Gaga performed on Doritos' Bold Stage at SXSW in Austin

Nov 24, 2013 ... Lady Gaga and R Kelly performed Do What U Want at the 2013 American Music Awards, Lady Gaga and R. Kelly

Lady Gaga: Born to be Free

Lady Gaga meets the Queen at the Royal Variety Performance in Blackpool

Lady Gaga and Sir Elton John at the white Tie and Tiara Ball in the U.K.

Lady Gaga—International Superstar

Lade Gaga with boyfriend Taylor Kinney (Chicago Fire actor)

Lady Gaga steals a kiss with boyfriend Taylor Kinney (Chicago Fire actor)

Lady Gaga: Born to be Free

Lady Gaga—drop dead chic

Lady Gaga poses in Versace spring-summer 2014 ad

Lady Gaga—International Superstar

Jan 20, 2014 ... Lady Gaga in Paris With Donatella Versace

Lady Gaga with Donatella Versace

Lady Gaga on the December 2013 Cover of Glamour Magazine

Lady Gaga on the Red Carpet

Lady Gaga—International Superstar

Lady Gaga - International Superstar And Entrepreneur

Lady Gaga with Perez Hilton

Lady Gaga promotes a new scent for women—Lady Gaga Fame Perfume by Lady Gaga

"I hope when I'm dead I'll be considered an icon."
—Lady Gaga to Larry King

"Success is not temporal. You either have it forever or you don't. My wealth is in the cultural impact I have and in my longevity and legacy and the stamp that I will leave on the universe."
—Lady Gaga to *The Guardian UK*

Conclusion

2014 and Beyond...

Back in 2009, NPR had declared that Lady Gaga was dangerous, quite simply, because her overnight success was "scary. She writes dangerously catchy songs that sound like nonsense but eat their way into your brain. She's always dressed in some combination of wigs, sunglasses and—if she wears much else—what looks like half a museum of modern art on her back. At the American Music Awards, she set her piano on fire and belted out a heart-wrenching ballad while smashing wine bottles on the keys. There's choreographed dancing in her videos, sure, but there are also wheelchairs and homicides, coffins and charred skeletons, the kinds of twisted and shaken visual imagery usually reserved for David Lynch films. She's a one-woman horror movie. We're just not used to turning on the TV and seeing performance art. Pop stars tend to be very straightforward; that's what makes them so likable, how easily they fit into one box or another. She's quite suddenly a very powerful woman in what's still a man's music industry."

Agreeing, her label CEO, Interscope head Jimmy Iovine offered his estimation in summing up Gaga's appeal that "artists like her are very rare. Artists that have that many facets of their career in line and can do that many things. She can write like Carole King, produce, sing like that, work-work-work like that. She gets her point of view across; she has the fashion, the performance—the entire vision. It's very, very rare. Only she can imagine it. I don't have that good of an imagination like she does. But she's the real thing. She will go as long as she wants to or physically can. Her talent will take her as far as she wants to take it. Most artists of this caliber, if they can stay healthy, there's no limitation. None."

This was clearly her intention looking to the future, with Gaga arguing to FT Magazine that "the beauty for me about being an artist is that the dream will never die because I'm not obsessed with material things and don't care about the money and don't care about the attention of the public but only the love of my fans. For me it's about keeping the dream alive of how much more devoted, how much more honest, how much better of an artist can I become? That's the only fear that I ever have, that the dream will die. I do see myself to be in an endless transformative state in the way that those performers you've mentioned were. I just am committed wholeheartedly to theatre with no intermission."

She treated fans in early 2014 to what Rolling Stone Magazine coined an "epic Artpop film" that ran 11 minutes and 46 seconds, and was directed by Gaga herself, demonstrating the firm hold of control she retained over the direction of Artpop's promotion, even when bringing in a big-name hotshot video director might have been the smarter play given the album's so-so sales thus far.

Though undeterred by the past, Gaga with her latest video clearly was taking aim at those suits she had gone through such an ugly public breakup with the previous winter, as RS described a backdrop where "the video opens to the strains of 'Artpop' with a scrum of men in suits fighting over money scattered on the ground. When the fray clears, Lady Gaga, dressed as a bird creature with tattered brown wings and a scarlet body, is left lying in their fight pit, where she's been pierced through with an arrow. She manages to makes her way to what at first appears to be a monastery, but the gates open onto a party mansion—Hearst Castle, actually. 'Venus' begins to play as Gaga is revived on the scene, baptized in the swimming pool and serenaded by a court orchestra of lipsynching Real Housewives of Beverly Hills. The 'film' switches gears again as the song shifts to 'G.U.Y.' and an invigorated Gaga, no longer winged, leads various male dance troupes in synchronized routines. There's also some kind of cloning going on (Gandhi and Michael Jackson, naturally) and suit made of Lego. Toward the end, Gaga and some female accomplices, dressed in confident black feathers, drive to an office building armed with crossbows, where they shoot money at the businessmen in the course of their hostile corporate takeover. The last four minutes of the film are taken up entirely by credits, to the tune of 'Manicure.' Gaga premiered the clip Saturday night on NBC's *Dateline* before making it available online."

Hitting the road that same spring to launch her ARTPOP world tour, Gaga's popularity among her fans demonstrated staying power in spite of her recent stumble at record stores, affirmed by Forbes.com's headline in March, 2014 that "six additional dates show demand is strong for Lady Gaga tickets and ArtPop Tour." Accompanied by an analysis of why Gaga may have landed on her feet after all, Forbes pointed to the fact that "after lackluster sales for the latest album 'Artpop'…amidst all the negative chatter, rumors have also been swirling that Lady Gaga tickets for her upcoming Artpop tour were suffering. The recent announcement of six additional shows are clear evidence that the tour is in good shape, and despite an album that didn't deliver as hoped, little monsters across the country want more…Live Nation reported that sales of Gaga concert tickets for North America and Europe are at 80% capacity sold, which is a strong number for a tour that is still two months from kicking off. According to Athur Fogel, Chairman of Live Nation's Global Touring division, the 29 shows that are on sale in North America have grossed $26 million in ticket sales so far, which averages to just under $1 million per show. With the additional six shows, gross revenue for the tour is now well north of $30 million…Given the resurgent demand for Lady Gaga tickets, it's clear that for established artists with a long history of success and legions of fans, one subpar album isn't enough to turn a tour like Artpop into a flop."

Dedicated to bringing fans a live concert event that "is the same whether I'm singing in front of 15,000 people in a big arena or a handful of people in a small club," Gaga shared with the Daily Mail UK of her live concert philosophy that "I play every show as if it were Madison Square Garden." By keeping her head up and her eyes on her fans and the future, the superstar clearly felt another key to her survival came with her constant focus on remaining "original," reasoning in a conversation with SHOWStudio.com that "*I think it's important…to strive for originality. I'm still working on it, I reference constantly: I've most recently felt that I've had some truly original moments. If you get one original moment in your career, you're solid. I push for that every day.*"

Putting that philosophy into action as she aimed for even higher heights than most pop stars ever dream, Gaga in late 2013 announced her plans to become among the first Millennium superstars to perform live in space, with the Hollywood Reporter revealing that "**her space voyage in 2015 involves two performances.** Gaga explained that she will perform on the spacecraft, simultaneously streamed at a concert at Ground Zero. Then she'll return and perform on the Ground Zero stage in person. 'Everyone that flies on Virgin Galactic is required to pay for their flight, and it's a trip to space, but they asked me and I don't have to pay for my flight, which is great, because it's mostly for rich people…I did not come this far to be afraid to go to space!'"

About the Author

Award-winning Music biographer Jake Brown has written 35 published books since 2001, featuring many authorized collaborations with some of rock's biggest artists, including 2013 Rock & Roll Hall of Fame inductees Heart (with Ann and Nancy Wilson), living guitar legend Joe Satriani, heavy metal pioneers Motorhead (with Lemmy Kilmister), late hip hop icon Tupac Shakur (with the estate), celebrated Rock drummer Kenny Aronoff, late Funk pioneer Rick James, superstar country music anthology 'Nashville Songwriter,' and the all-star rock producers anthology Behind the Boards, among many others. Brown has also appeared as the featured biographer of record on Fuse TV's Live Through This series and Bloomberg TV's Game Changers series, and received national press in USA Today, MTV.com, and Billboard, etc. In 2012, Brown won the Association for Recorded Sound Collections Awards in the category of Excellence in Historical Recorded Sound Research.

ORDER FORM
WWW.AMBERBOOKS.COM

Fax Orders: 480-283-0991
Telephone Orders: 602-743-7211
Postal Orders: Send Checks & Money Orders Payable to:
    Amber Books
    1334 E. Chandler Blvd., Suite 5-D67, Phoenix, AZ 85048
Online Orders: E-mail: Amberbk@aol.com

____*Lady Gaga: Born to Be Free*, ISBN#: 978-1-937269-44-9 $15.00
____*Beyoncé Before the Legend*, ISBN #: 978-1-937269-42-5, $12.00
____*Kanye West Before the Legend*, ISBN #: 978-1-937269-40-1, $5.00
____*Nicki Minaj: The Woman Who Stole the World*, ISBN #: 978-1-937269-30-2, $12.00
____*Eminem & The Detroit Rap Scene*, ISBN#: 978-1-937269-26-5, $15.00
____*Too Young to Die, Too Old to Live: The Amy Winehouse Story*, ISBN#: 978-1-937269-28-9, $15.00
____*Lil Wayne: An Unauthorized Biography*, ISBN#: 978-0-9824922-3-7, $15.00
____*Black Eyed Peas: Unauthorized Biography*, ISBN#: 978-0-9790976-4-5, $16.95
____*Red Hot Chili Peppers: In the Studio*, ISBN #: 978-0-9790976-5-2, $16.95
____*Dr. Dre In the Studio*, ISBN#: 0-9767735-5-4, $16.95
____*Tupac Shakur—(2Pac) In The Studio*, ISBN#: 0-9767735-0-3, $16.95
____*Jay-Z…and the Roc-A-Fella Dynasty*, ISBN#: 0-9749779-1-8, $16.95
____*Ready to Die: Notorious B.I.G.*, ISBN#: 0-9749779-3-4, $16.95
____*Suge Knight: The Rise, Fall, and Rise of Death Row Records*, ISBN#: 0-9702224-7-5, $21.95
____*50 Cent: No Holds Barred*, ISBN#: 0-9767735-2-X, $16.95
____*Aaliyah—An R&B Princess in Words and Pictures*, ISBN#: 0-9702224-3-2, $10.95
____*You Forgot About Dre: Dr. Dre & Eminem*, ISBN#: 0-9702224-9-1, $10.95
____*Michael Jackson: The King of Pop*, ISBN#: 0-9749779-0-X, $29.95

Name:_____

Company Name:_____

Address:_____

City:_____State:_____Zip:_____

Telephone: (_____)_____E-mail:_____

For Bulk Rates Call: 602-743-7211   ORDER NOW

Lady GaGa	$15.00	❑ Check ❑ Money Order ❑ Cashiers Check
Beyoncé	$12.00	❑ Credit Card: ❑ MC ❑ Visa ❑ Amex ❑ Discover
Kanye West	$15.00	
Eminem	$15.00	CC#_____
The Amy Winehouse Story	$15.00	Expiration Date:_____
Nicki Minaj	$12.00	
Lil Wayne: An Unauthorized Biography	$15.00	**Payable to: Amber Books**
Black Eyed Peas	$16.95	Mail to: Amber Books
Red Hot Chili Peppers	$16.95	1334 E. Chandler Blvd., Suite 5-D67
Dr. Dre In the Studio	$16.95	Phoenix, AZ 85048
Tupac Shakur	$16.95	**Shipping:** $5.00. Allow 7 days for delivery.
Jay-Z…	$16.95	
Ready to Die: Notorious B.I.G.,	$16.95	
Suge Knight:	$21.95	**Total enclosed:** $_____
50 Cent: No Holds Barred,	$16.95	
Aaliyah—An R&B Princess	$10.95	
Dr. Dre & Eminem	$10.95	
Michael Jackson: The King of Pop	$29.95	

CPSIA information can be obtained at www.ICGtesting.com
Printed in the USA
LVOW06s2128170815

450451LV00032B/2239/P

9 781937 269449